CW01511082

An Ordinary Life

My 1960s Childhood in Hull

by Julie Hall

Dedication

With heart-felt thanks to the memory of our devoted parents.

Mum : Sylvia Ann Clappison (nee Arton) – 19th May 1935 to 19th May 2019

Dad : Geoffrey Priestley Clappison – 15th March 1932 to 13th November 2019

Always loved. Forever missed.

And to the memory of our adored and inspirational son Joshua Alan Hall – 14th November 1990 to 16th July 2015. No words can express what you meant to us. We console our hearts with this thought: *the souls of the righteous are in the hand of God* from the Wisdom of Solomon, Chapter 3, Verse 1. We will meet again at His throne.

Contents

Introduction

The old saying goes that "Everyone has one book in them". If that is true, then this is mine. I always wanted to write a book concerning my early childhood days in Hull but I never seemed to have the time and then, all of a sudden, I did have the time, thanks to Covid and several lock-downs.

I needed to distract myself from the horrors of the pandemic. From the switch-back ride of death statistics, from the fear, from our own Covid ill-health and the general boredom of being confined to house and garden all day and every day. I even became too scared to take my one-hour daily exercise allowance due to the number of people walking past our corner-sited house. Our Church, our Bible study and book group all closed down. These were the sources of my spiritual and social life. During that time, we hardly saw anyone at all except our family members, the postman and the delivery drivers.

During that time, I started to think about what I wanted to leave as a legacy to my remaining children. Life for children and young people now is so very different from the lives we enjoyed in Hull. I wanted to write down a record of that time. I also wanted it to be the record of a very ordinary 1960s childhood, of a united, happy (mostly) family and to be an elegy for a lost place and a lost time.

Leaving Hull at the tender age of 10 was heart-breaking for me. Looking back to a time before we left was a total joy. However, I need to acknowledge the fact that these memories are mine and mine alone. As our late great Queen Elizabeth once famously said, "Recollections may vary". So, I wish to record (particularly if you are one of the family) that some of the things I have written here may not chime with things as you remember them. Perhaps the dates are a little different or some of the incidents included may not have happened as you recall them. I can only apologise and hope that you can forgive any discrepancies. After all, I was only a little girl at the time and I am describing things as I believe they happened to me and also from what I was told by members of the family. And I hope that what I have written will perhaps interest, amuse and bring back memories of happy times in people's lives that have almost disappeared. This is my first book of memories: a legacy for my children and generations of our family still to come. I hope that the reader will find something of enjoyment and amusement as a well as a little of the darker side of life. I trust you will enjoy what I have committed to paper.

Julie Hall

January 2025

My Very First Childhood Memory

My very first childhood memory: I am lying on my back in my big navy blue 'Silver Cross' pram in the garden of 28 Beech Avenue, Garden Village, Hull. I have just awoken from a nap, and I am kicking my legs and waving my arms in joy. There is a special white embroidery anglaise sunshade over my head which is attached to the pram; it keeps me cool and stops the sun catching my delicate skin. I have kicked off my thin wool blanket. The blanket is woven in multi-coloured checks of pale blue, pink and cream. Two young women are peering at me over the sides of the pram. Both are pretty and smiling and cooing at me. One is my lovely mum, the other is my Auntie Fay, mum's sister who is 10 years younger than her, so she was just a young teenager at this time. It is a very warm sunny day and, in the background, I can hear chiming – it must be the church bells of our local church, St Columba's. I can see the leaves on our only garden tree fluttering in the gentle breeze. This is the start of all the memories of my childhood days in Hull.

The look of love
Mum and Dad's Wedding Day
24th March 1956.

From left to right (back row): Grandma, Granddad, Malcolm Wykes (Dad's Best Man), Mum and Dad, Pop and Nanna, (front row): bridesmaids Nita and Fay.

CHAPTER 1 : Birth and Before

I was born Julie Clappison on the 8th December 1958 in my paternal grandparents' front room – their *best* room – reserved for Christmas and entertaining and, of course, specially prepared for my birth. We were a working-class family living in Hull and I was my parents' first-born child, weighing in at just over 6lbs. My dad said that when he held me for the first time, my face was all screwed up, angry and red. I suppose I was the first new-born baby he had ever held, so he had no other child to compare me to. He himself was an only child. My grandparents had hoped to have a large family, but they were only blessed with my dad and, being so incredibly modest, my grandma would never have dreamed of consulting her family doctor on so intimate a matter, so she poured all her love and devotion into my dad instead.

Everyone in my family must have rejoiced at my birth though I am pretty sure they would have been hoping for a boy as, in those faraway days, this was the ultimate child-bearing prize. My mother's dad, 'Pop', certainly would have wanted a grandson. He used to call his three daughters "a load of long-hairs".

Anyway, for better or worse, there I was. Born at 63 Lodge Street in a city still recovering from extensive wartime bombing and destruction. The Nazis had been trying to starve us into submission by bombing the port where most of the food came in. There were still plenty of bomb sites left from the Second World War and it took many years to put things right in the city.

I was born just in time for dinner, 12.30, and I never missed a meal for the rest of my childhood. Dinner was always a hot home-cooked meal, but on the occasion of my birth, Grandma had popped to the corner shop for Birdseye chicken pies, one of the few ready-made convenience foods at that time. I still love them today.

There was some discussion over what I should be named. Grandad liked the name 'Yvonne', no one else did though, so that was out. It has always astonished me that Mum and Dad never had a clear idea before our births as to what any of their three children might be called. Mum said she wanted names that could not be shortened, so she preferred shorter names. She did not give any of us a middle name, which was a great disappointment to me as all my friends had what they called 'secret' names, all except our family, of course.

Both Mum and Dad were massive film and musical theatre fans and in the end they settled on 'Julie' after Julie Andrews, a hugely popular singer appearing in musicals at the time. She was in *My Fair Lady* where she was a massive hit with her melodious soprano voice. In 1957 she was on Broadway in that show and then in 1958 - the year of my birth - she started to do the same show in London in May. Julie Andrews had been a child performer, going on to success with numerous films and shows (probably *The Sound of Music* being the best loved), but with a long career stretching into her eighties. I have never really liked my name; it was quite common in my childhood and at one time there were three Julies in my school class. I guess those parents had the same idea as mine. Dad's cousin, on the other hand, was so impressed by Mum and Dad naming us Julie and Neil (my younger-by-two-years brother) that he asked

7

Dad if he could name his daughter Julie and later, his son Neil. Dad said, "Of course" so there was another relative named after Julie Andrews in our extended family. However, he changed his mind about the name Neil and called his son John instead. As I said, my family seemed to have problems naming their children.

The family I had most to do with were, of course, my mum and dad ("Daddy and Mummy" when I was young), Dad's parents, Grandad Albert and Grandma Margery, Nana (Mum's mum) Gertrude and Pop (Mum's dad) Frank and, of course, my Aunties Fay and Nita (Mum's much younger sisters). Mum was 10 when Fay was born and 11 when Nita came along. The huge gap was down to two things: firstly, the war, "You couldn't have children in the war," Pop always said, "you didn't know what was going to happen from one day to the next!"

My mum was only four when the war began and Nana's deep desire for a second child had to wait until the war was over. Then, becoming pregnant and carrying a baby to full term was a problem for Nana and she had painful and emotionally difficult miscarriages. My mum saw all this and was like a little mum to her own mother. Nana and Pop were happy and, no doubt, relieved to have another daughter after my mum. However, when Nana then had Nita a year later, Pop declared, "I was in the dog-'ouse then!" Whoops.

I remember Pop telling me how he had first met and fallen in love with Nana. He and a friend had gone to Hull Fair, one of the biggest fairs in the country. They had arranged to meet two girls there, but they soon realised that the girls had stood them up. They decided to look for another couple of girls to enjoy their evening with instead, and one of them was my nana. Although they were both very young, Pop told me that they had quickly known that they were meant to be together for the rest of their lives.

They both loved ballroom dancing and used to enjoy going to different venues to dance during their courtship. Scarborough and Blackpool were particular favourite places for them. They also enjoyed going to the musical theatre and to the cinema together. As they sat in the darkness of the cinema one night during a particularly romantic film, Pop whispered in Nana's ear, "I want to give you a baby." Nana said it sent a shiver from the top of her head to the tips of her toes. One night, when Pop and Nana were staying in a Scarborough boarding house – in separate rooms, of course – Nana tapped on Pop's door; she was nervous, but very excited. Pop said she offered herself to him as they were deeply in love. Pop said he gently turned her down as he knew they would be taking a massive risk in making love without the benefit of being married.

Pop and Nana were very different characters. Pop was very tough and was a dominating husband and father; he definitely ruled the roost and what he said went. In common with a lot of working-class husbands of the era, he expected his wife to serve him first in every way. Their roles in life were clearly defined: the husband went out to work to earn money to support the family; the wife stayed at home looking after the house and children. Housework and child-rearing in those days were definitely full-time jobs with no labour-saving machines to get the chores done quickly. There were few nurseries or play

9

groups for pre-school children and mums relied on their own mothers for a much-needed break from their children. Nana shopped every day for fresh ingredients to prepare meals as there were no fridges or freezers invented at that time.

Nana, in her later years (when the children had all left home), fancied taking a little job at the small supermarket at the top of the street to earn herself what was called in those days 'pin money' for her personal spending. Pop's response to Nana was, "When you start working, I'll give up!" It was thought to be a disgrace for a working-class man to have a wife he could not keep financially.

Pop had a very morbid side to him and his stories of sudden and unexpected death gleaned as a police officer kept me awake at night. As a baby, Pop himself had not been expected to live, saying he was the 'runt of the litter'. So weak and sickly was he at birth that the doctor advised his mother to "throw him in the dustbin". Ironically, Pop outlived his other siblings and died at the age of 82.

Pop was also a very sentimental man, often giving way to tears – very unusual in a man of that era – and given to displays of overt affection, kissing and cuddling Nana quite openly. I thought they were the most romantic couple I had ever seen. My mother knew better. "It's all fuss and clart" was her tart observation. She knew the true story.

Nana was a beautiful woman. We have many photos of her dressed in flapper-style clothes in the 1920s, very fashionable, and she was always smartly turned out. Nana had dark brown hair and huge dark eyes, a gentle nature and she used makeup to make the best of herself. Nana had been brought up in the countryside and she used to escape Hull during the worst of the bombing, staying with her mum and dad Crane in Bilton. Of course, she took Sylvia (my mum) with her and due to the war, my mum started school a year late and at six years old.

My nana was always a bit afraid of Pop; he had an explosive temper. All his family found him scary at times. If his dinner was not on the table right on the dot at 5.30, he would throw it at the wall. I understand that he also used to hit his wife and daughter on occasions – sadly, not unusual for those days – although I was confused when I learned that as Pop used to say constantly to me that he would never dream of beating his wife like he saw his dad beating his own mother. Or perhaps that was the guilt talking.

As a child, I used to stare at my nana's lovely face and wonder why her mouth constantly moved in a nervous tic. Perhaps fear of provoking Pop's anger might have been partly to blame. Nana did not always accept things quietly, however: during their courtship they were walking past a high-class leather shop in Hull. She was arm-in-arm with Pop when she spotted a beautiful, but out of her price range, handbag. A few days later, Pop went back to buy it for her, but it had already been sold, so he chose a bag he thought looked similar and took it to her as a gift of love. Nana, however, did not like the substitute bag, told

11

him so and slammed the door in his face. When her father heard of her rejection of the gift, he called Pop back and made her apologise to him on the doorstep.

My mother told me that one day, just before Christmas, Nana was grumbling about all the extra work she had to do towards the festive season, so Pop decided to help out. While she was out Christmas shopping, Pop got lots of cheap tinsel and glitter decorations which he and the girls hung all through the downstairs rooms in the house. Instead of being pleased at this well-intentioned gesture, Nana hit the roof saying the decorations looked cheap and nasty. She would not stop nagging him until Pop had taken them all down.

My dad's parents, Grandma and Grandad, could hardly have been more different to Nana and Pop. They had met at Church (Portabella Road Methodist Church). Grandad had come to play the cornet for a guest band at one of the services and they began their courtship from there. Both of them were committed Christians and I remember Grandma reading her Bible and praying every day after dinnertime. They always went to Church on Sundays and some other times as well – in fact, their social life was all conducted at Church, apart from time spent with their neighbours on their street. However, later on in life, they stopped attending the Methodist Church and started going to East Park Baptist Church instead. The minister at the Methodist Church lost several of his congregation after an inflammatory sermon in which he declared that he did not want 'oncers' at his Church on Sundays, only those who would commit to going to both morning and evening services. He got what he asked for.

Grandma was an archetypal, loving, cuddly grandmother. A large lady who could not care less about how she looked; she had never had her long grey hair cut in her life and she plaited it and coiled it at the nape of her neck every day. She had little interest in clothes and no interest at all in makeup. Her only vanity being a small tube of Veloutée powdered cream which she smoothed onto her cheeks if she was going out to the shops.

Very suspicious of electricity, she always warmed up old fashioned irons on the fire to smooth out the creases on the family's clothes and she was usually to be found cooking in their tiny kitchen or sewing or mending for my mum. Mum hated mending but Grandma was happy to do it for her.

Grandma was the best grandmother any child could have because she absolutely adored us and would do anything to make us happy. Although Grandma and Grandad had very little money to spare, they spent what they had on little toys, colouring books, magic painting books, anything they thought we might enjoy playing with, and they always had time to spend with us and found everything we did and said to be interesting, entertaining and remarkably intelligent. We always knew they were totally committed to our lives and welfare and never ever told us off or smacked us. In fact, Grandma did not believe in physical discipline at all, which was unusual in those days. Dad had never been physically chastised by his parents, although he had been caned several times at school...

Grandma had the kindest, friendliest disposition; everyone she knew loved her because she would help anyone in need, including stray cats who found a ready spot in her home. Cats were one of her dearest loves and I well remember how she would stroke and fuss any cats we came across in the neighbourhood – so much so that they even used to follow her down the streets as we continued on our walks. I certainly inherited my love of cats from her.

Grandma made every walk and every visit special and fun. She loved celebration days: birthdays, Christmases, Easter, and she went out of her way to create memories around those times so that we would remember them for a lifetime.

Grandad too was a wonderful grandparent. He loved telling us all about the world in which we lived; much of it was self-taught as he spent too much of his childhood dodging school. He hated school so he used to hide his school clothes up the chimney, so he did not have to go. The only day of the week he really wanted to go was Wednesday because on Wednesday afternoons the school did an art class and it was the only thing he, Albert, was interested in. Grandad loved his art and he spent a lot of his retirement drawing and painting – he even joined an art class. He was happy that Neil and I were interested and he shared his skills with us. He used to tell us that he often got in trouble with his dad as his father used to take his belt off to beat him with. His mother used to shield him under her voluminous skirts and she used to take the beating intended for her son. It seems that physical punishment was the norm in working-class families in the early years of the 20th century.

Grandad and I both had birthdays in December. I was meant to have been born on Christmas Day but arrived on the 8th December instead. Grandad's birthday was the 15th December. He never got a present on that day, being told he had to wait until Christmas as there was no spare money for treats so near the festive season. He told me that one year, when he had been particularly naughty, he had a stocking from Father Christmas which held only coal. Other years, he received a stocking which contained a shiny new penny, some pencils or crayons, a small colouring book and a small toy, such as tin toy steam train, some penny sweets and there was always an orange in the toe. For him, this was magical – the only childhood presents he ever received. No wonder Christmas was so eagerly anticipated by poorer children in those days. Families were often large; only the father worked, usually for poor wages and he would often keep most of the money for his own pleasure, leaving mother to scrimp and save for any little extras for Christmas for the children. As Grandad used to say, Neil and I were very lucky to have all the toys and games we were given.

Baby days with Mum
and Dad in East Park.

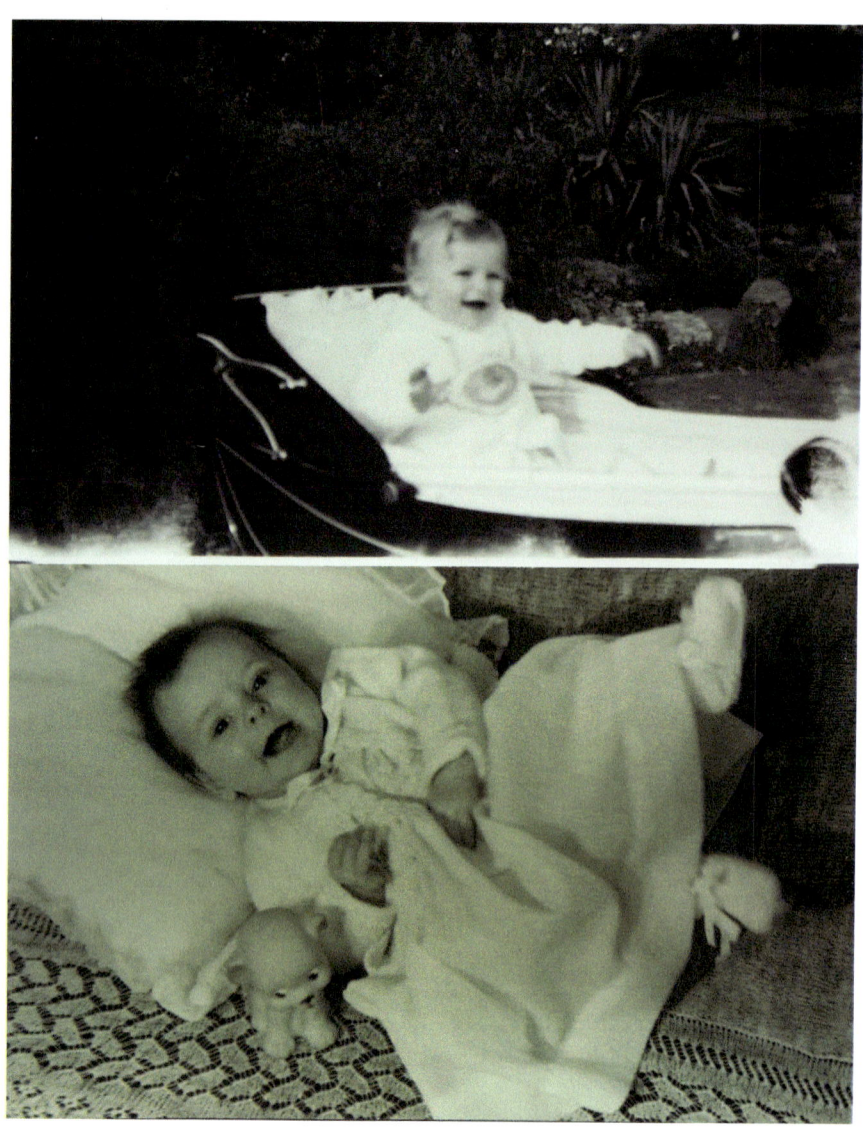

Top: me in my pram, in East Park (I look very happy!)

Bottom: A professional photo taken by a photographer friend of Dad's.

CHAPTER 2 : Our Lovely Parents

My mum, Sylvia Ann Arton, lived with her parents, Pop and Nana, and later her younger sisters Fay and Nita, at 50 Shaftsbury Avenue. It was about a mile or so away from Dad's house. Mum knew of Dad from an early age. Children were sent outside to play in the neighbourhood and most people knew many other families as people tended not to move around back in those days. Dad, Geoffrey, was in a gang of boys and they could be quite mischievous, getting up to all sorts of naughty tricks. Specialities for them included apple scrumping (stealing to you and me), dirtying old ladies' huge knickers on the washing line by throwing balls of mud into them, knocking on doors then running away, and frightening the local learning-disabled girl by dressing up in sheets and pretending to be ghostly apparitions – the poor girl was terrified!

Dad always said that the war years were the most exciting years of his life as he and the gang roamed free. Bombsites were their playgrounds, despite the obvious danger, and Dad amassed an extensive collection of shrapnel. Once, he even found a leather glove with a hand in it, the remains, no doubt, of a German fighter pilot. Add to that the fact that, due to his parents' anxieties about the bombing, they slept every night of the war in the Anderson shelter at the bottom of the garden, my dad was basically feral for five years. No wonder Mum's parents told her to "stay away from *that* boy".

Like Dad, our mum was effectively an only child for 10 years and the fact that her parents had forbidden her from mixing with Dad and his gang might have made him even more attractive to her. And attractive, he was – he was tall, slim with blue eyes and white-blond hair. People used to say that, as a young man, he had the look of Prince Philip about him.

My mum too was very pretty – she had huge brown eyes, dark hair and had a very sweet smile. Like Nana in her youth, she liked clothes and was interested in fashion. She used to work at Hammonds Department Store. She worked for a while in the sports department, then moved to the baby department. Her claim to fame there was serving the Beverley sisters (Britain's answer to the Andrew sisters) when one of them was expecting her first child. Being quite tall and beautiful, she used to do modelling for some of the women's fashions which she greatly enjoyed.

My dad started his career as a booking clerk in Paragon Street Station, Hull. It was not what he really wanted to do. He was a very clever man and longed, alongside some of his friends at Malet Lambert Grammar School, to enter the Sixth Form and go, eventually, to university. However, there was no chance of that as his parents could never have afforded for him to go. I was, in fact, the first person in my family to go on to higher education and to get a degree.

Working-class children in my dad's day had to go to work at an early age, so Dad began his long career on the railways at the age of 16. As well as selling train tickets, sorting mail and parcels, he had to keep the older men well supplied with hot drinks, as well as climbing up on a stepladder every day to ensure the station clock was wound properly and telling the correct time, which was very important to the station.

Dad and his parents were always in East Park Baptist Church and Mum's parents occasionally attended also. The biggest draw though for the young people at Church was the youth group. There were not many activities provided for young people in those days, apart from by the Church, and in an age without TV, video or the internet, many teenagers went to Churches for their social life.

My mum first started noticing Dad as a prospective romantic partner at the youth club when she was about 15. She had already been courted by another young man, a Roman Catholic who lived around the corner from her. It had been encouraged by the boy's mother who said Sylvia had the look of the Virgin Mary. Dad too had had a previous girlfriend but it had ended quickly and in embarrassment for Geoff. He had taken this young lady, Diane, out to the pictures and had bought them a bag of sweets to share. The film was a sad one and, to Geoff's horror, Diane had been overwhelmed by tears at the ending. This caused her to drop the bag of sweets all over the cinema floor and Dad spent quite a while scrambling about to pick up all the sweets. Dad never could stand the sight of a woman crying, not to mention his humiliation at trying to retrieve the lost sweets in the dark. Dad broke off the relationship and Diane ended up going out with his good friend, Mike, instead and they later got married.

My mum was made of much stronger stuff than Diane. She hardly ever cried, and certainly not at a sad film. Dad always used to say that Mum had 'thrown herself' at him, which seemed a bit unlikely knowing Mum's shy and retiring nature. Or perhaps she instinctively knew that Dad was the one for her.

He was certainly a fine-looking, sporty type of young man and he loved to run, attend Rugby League (Hull Kingston Rovers) and he played in the Church cricket team for several years. He won silver cups!

As their families vaguely knew each other, Sylvia had every reason to seek him out and to ask after his parents, and then, along came the perfect opportunity for Sylvia and Geoffrey to spend more time together on an almost daily basis. East Park Baptist Church decided that Easter celebrations that year would be enhanced by the production of a play all about the very first Easter. All the young people were excited about it and auditioned for the various parts on offer. Dad was always a good speaker and he was given the part of Pontius Pilate. He had to ask the crowd whether he should release Barabbas (a notorious robber and murderer), or Jesus, who was totally innocent but who had got on the wrong side of the Jewish religious authorities. When the crowd was baying for Jesus to be crucified, Pilate then washed his hands to show that he did not agree that Jesus should be murdered. The part of the servant girl who brought in the bowl and towel for Pontius Pilate to wash his hands was given to my mum and, as I often thought to myself, Mum was his much-loved serving girl forever after. I am certain that the Easter play was the perfect start to Mum and Dad's burgeoning romance.

Both families seemed happy about the match, but Pop was not, especially when he learned how quickly they wished to marry. Mum wanted to marry before her 21st birthday and because parents were allowed to withhold their consent before then, that is what Pop did. Despite Mum's fear of Pop,

Mum was determined to get her way on this – the most important day of her life. In the end, she won.

Sylvia and Geoff married on the 24th March (before the end of the tax year, as most working class couples did) at East Park Baptist Church in 1956. It was quite a big do with lots of relatives and friends invited. Nita and Fay looked adorable dressed in Bo Peep bonnets and long dresses, holding fur-trimmed muffs to keep their hands warm – well, it was only March! The wedding took place in the Church with the meal in the Church Hall. The photos (of which there were many) look at if everyone had a truly happy day. Mum and Dad looked so young and innocent in those photos and, after my dad died, we came across a brown envelope containing a booklet, sent by a friend who had married earlier, about what to expect on your wedding night. In common with most of Dad's friends, that book must have been eagerly read and digested before the honeymoon. However, my mum's only remark to me about honeymoons was "and honeymoons are not all they're cracked up to be either". Nevertheless, that happy and convivial wedding day led to my birth three years later.

Me as a toddler at Malcolm and Barbara Wykes' house at St Albans. Their daughter Jill was a few months older than me, though we never got on!

My doting Aunties. Fay (left) and Nita on Filey beach.

CHAPTER 3 : My Little Brother

For two and a half years, I was the only child on both sides of my family. I basked in their adoration and encouragement. Every week, Grandma and Grandad visited at least for one morning to give my mum a break by taking me out in my big pram, and later, in my smaller pushchair. Also, Aunties Fay and Nita often visited; they were teenagers, but they seemed very old to me. Fay especially was a very gentle and maternal girl and she loved taking me out on her days off from work. We used to go to East Park a lot as it was our nearest green space. East Park was a very large park with a huge duck pond, floral displays and swings and slides. It was a perfect place to visit with children. I sometimes wonder how many hours I spent feeding a great variety of ducks, geese and swans with stale pieces of bread whilst also snacking on them myself. I particularly loved the cold, sunny autumn days in the park as, due to the large number of trees, there were many piles of leaves to crunch through, collect or throw. For a child, East Park seemed magical.

One particularly cold winter, the entire lake froze over and Dad, Neil and I walked almost to the gates of Malet Lambert Grammar School over the ice. Malet Lambert was Dad's old school, just about the best academically in Hull. "You'll go there one day!" he used to tell me confidently. I did not like the look of it myself – large, old fashioned and forbidding and, of course, I never did get there as by the time I was old enough for secondary school, we had moved to York.

Being the only child brought some high expectations with it. I was bright and also rather precocious, encouraged particularly by Dad. This did cause a bit of friction. Pop (who liked the female sex to know their place) was not at all impressed by my way of showing off to visitors. He was concerned that I would one day rule the roost and expressed his thoughts to Mum and Dad. "By the time that girl's 16, if she carries on like this, she'll have you out of the house", he declared. My dad was furious with Pop and they almost came to blows over me. Mum was terrified and stepped in to mediate and bring about peace. Dad backed down, realising that he would never win over Pop, as his womenfolk were afraid of him and wanted harmony in the family.

Mum was always harder on me and my behaviour than Dad was. Strictly brought up herself, she wanted her children to be as good as she had been as a child. Dad, on the other hand, had been given a lot more freedom to be himself as a child and he liked to see his children's talents and their expression of their individuality. It caused quite a few problems over our childhood upbringing.

After two and half years of being the only child, it was a shock of massive proportions to discover that I now had a baby brother. Neil (again, no middle name) was born on 3rd May 1961. Again, he was born in Grandma and Grandad's front room, attended by the local midwife. Neil must have been my parents' (especially Mum's) dream baby come true: blond and beautiful like Dad, placid, lovely-natured, but, most of all, male. He was everything parents in those far-off days longed for and, for Mum, she had done what her mum had not been able to do for Pop; she had given Dad a son and everything that went along with that. A son, to follow in his footsteps, go to rugby and cricket with, play snooker with – in other words, a playmate for Dad. No wonder I felt shaken by the new order in our family. All the attention that had been focused upon me appeared to be turned upon this tiny upstart in a carrycot. At least, that is how it appeared to me. And even now, I remember how displaced I felt, how jealous and full of hate. Nothing now would ever be the same and I just had to get on with it and become something new – a big sister. I soon realised that being naughty, tantrumming and disagreeable would do no good at all. Perhaps, on the other hand, being a loving, concerned sibling would do the trick - to bring back the 'old days'.

On several occasions, Mum found me pretending to rock Neil gently to sleep but it took her a while to realise that I had actually woken him up beforehand by biting his fingers. It was war and the war continued off and on for quite some time with, every now and again, a huge and painful physical battle. It took me quite some time to see Neil as an ally and a friend and I do not think that really happened until I had to stay in hospital when I was five and I realised that I was actually going to miss Neil whilst I was away.

Dad's photographer friend once again came to take some family photos. This time Neil was definitely the star attraction!

My baby brother Neil has arrived. My face says it all!

In the garden at 28 Beech Avenue. Mum looks radiant
I look like I'm trying to make the best of it…….

A happy day in the garden
of 28 Beech Avenue with
my best playmate, Dad.
In this picture on the
right, I have him all to
myself.

CHAPTER 4 : School Days

Mum found Neil and I quite a handful at home. Housework was incredibly demanding in the early 1960s, although we did have a washing machine by then. Mum and Dad were not able to afford one before I was born, even washing the sheets in the bath by hand when she was first married. So, Mum had a washing machine, but it did not resemble the ones we use nowadays: it needed to be filled up via a hosepipe attached to a tap, the powder was put in the drum from the top and the washer agitated the clothing. It then needed emptying and filling up with rinsing water and after that the cleaned, rinsed clothing or sheets were pushed manually through rollers on the top (a 'built-in mangle') to squeeze out all the moisture before the washing could be dried out, ironed and put away. It was almost a full-time job and Mum worked hard doing the washing for the whole of her life. As a small child, I recall the shelf in the kitchen where there was always an array of different washing powders as Mum experimented in her quest to find the cleanest wash – was it Daz, Persil, Omo or Lux Flakes? She also used green washing soap to aid her handwashing, of which there was still a great deal, especially Dad's shirt collars and cuffs.

Now, with Neil, there were always buckets of nappies soaking in Milton. Disposable nappies were many years away. Little wonder that mums started holding their babies over potties from a few weeks old to get them toilet trained as quickly as possible. Most 1960s' babies were fully trained in using a potty and out of nappies by around the one-year mark. It would be quite a while before the psychologists pointed out that this rushed potty-training might have mental health implications for the baby involved. Early potty-training was one of the main traits of a successful mother, closely followed by her baby being a good four-hourly feeder with a healthy weight and an ability to sleep soundly all through the night. Daytime napping outside in the big pram was also encouraged as being healthy – a technique still utilised in the 1990s for my own children – it really does work because the fresh air lulls the baby to sleep.

I am sure that both Mum and Dad were excited at the prospect of me starting school. I could not wait myself; all I wanted to do was to learn to read. Reading was very important to us as a family. As a child, Dad had never been allowed to join a library. As Dad was an only child, Grandma had been terrified of germs, and she saw library books as being contaminated. Dad wore a Foxes golden locket around his neck to ward off germs, but Grandma thought that borrowing books would even circumvent that precaution. She kept Dad off school for two years between the ages of five and seven due to a mastoid on his ear. I do not think it was entirely about his health. I think Grandma preferred him to be at home, keeping him close to her. It certainly worked as he adored her. However, once an adult, Dad wasted no time in joining the local library. His favourite books were thrillers, especially Agatha Christie thrillers; he read every one of her books.

There was a lovely little library in the square of shops in Garden Village where we were fortunate to live. He got me library tickets when I was four years old, and I was allowed to choose my own books even before I was able to read them. Dad always had a newspaper delivered every morning (The Daily Mail) and when we went to Grandma and Grandad's, we read their Daily Express also. Reading the newspapers also became a daily preoccupation for myself from the age of about nine. Grandad also got Readers Digest and Grandma got Woman's Realm magazine, so I also read those and often cut out pictures for my scrapbook.

There was much discussion about which school I should attend. Most children who lived on the Garden Village estate went to the dark Victorian primary school a short walk away. My mum, however, considered it 'rough' and she wanted something better for me. At that time, Grandad had become the caretaker at Archbishop William Temple Church of England Primary School about a mile away from where we lived. It was a newly built school intended for mainly Christian families after the Church revival in the post-war era. One storey, modern with lighted airy classrooms, it was spoken of highly by my grandparents, especially for its peaceful Christian ethos. That school was Mum's choice; Dad was not so sure, "Too much religion and not enough learning", was his verdict. Mum, in this case, prevailed. I recall sitting for my pre-school interview in Miss Mackrell (the headmistress') office. She asked if I was looking forward to going to school, I said, "Yes." "What are you most looking forward to doing at school?" she asked. "Reading", I said.

Reading was a little bit different at my school, we discovered. They used a progressive modern method called 'ITA', the initial teaching alphabet. It had been developed by James Pitman who invented shorthand as a means of speeding up the early days of learning to read. I do not think it ever caught on generally as a reading teaching method as children had to transition to normal reading books at about the age of seven. It was the transition that many pupils found difficult, including Neil, who never really enjoyed reading as a child because of that. I, on the other hand, was highly motivated and I quickly learned the ITA system and had no problems moving on to read real books. I was also good at writing, although not handwriting. I loved creative writing, poetry, drama and movement to music. However, I hated maths and later science, right from my earliest school days and I was never any good at either subject. As a trainee teacher, I had to take a basic maths test each year in college and each year, I got just one more point than required to continue my training. Nowadays, I would not be allowed to train as I did not get good enough GCE maths results. That is how baffled I have always been by maths.

I did love school though, and I loved *most* of my teachers and I had lots of friends. Yes, we did do a fair amount of scripture, which I enjoyed, and our teachers were all Christians. On holy days, we all walked two-by-two to St Columba's Church where we worshipped in the beautiful building where Nana and Pop had married years before. It had a very distinctive smell: incense, perhaps? It was quite a High Church, and the front wall had a massive larger-than-life painting of Jesus calling fishermen Andrew and Simon Peter to follow him. I used to spend hours studying that picture. I loved my Church going, believed in God completely, and even better, after the service, our mums were there to take us home for lunch and the afternoon, because holy days were also half-day holidays. We had quite a few of those, although our mums were not quite as pleased as we were.

As we lived quite a long way from school, at first, Mum used to put Neil in the pushchair and take me there, then it was back for dinner at home; I never stayed for school dinners. Dad would come home on his bike, and we ate a hot meal at dinnertime. As Mum had to prepare dinner, I quickly became used to doing all the journeys on my own. I used to walk around in a daze, and I nearly got knocked down by a car one day; I was not looking at the usually quiet road. The man driving shouted at me, swore and shook his fist. I never forgot to check the roads again, even the quietest ones. Mum and Dad would have had a fit if they had known that their only daughter might not have reached the age of seven.

The walk to and from school could be quite eventful. When Neil joined school at five, I was in charge of getting us there and back safely. We had quite a long walk to and from school and, when I revisited Garden Village in the 1990s, I was still able to find my way there and back on foot, even though I had not been back there for 30 years.

Getting to school without getting dog mess on my shoes was a major issue. We had to cross 'the Oval' which, as the name suggests, was a large open green space in an oval shape and many of my walks across there left me with dirty, smelly shoes, which needed to be cleaned with paper towels before I could go into assembly. The weather was often unpleasant and we might arrive at school or home soaked to the skin. The worst weather we encountered was fog. This being Hull and near to the North Sea, 'pea souper' fogs used to regularly roll in. One day, coming home from school, we could hardly see our hands in front of our faces. The noises of the cars on the busy main road were muffled and made it dangerous to cross. That was one frightening walk home! Again, on dreadfully windy days, it sometimes felt as though the wind might pick us up and carry us away, especially Neil who was very small and slight for his age. We were buffeted to and fro and felt exhausted by journey's end. All this, and the school bell tolling, reminded us that when it stopped, we were late. It was a genuine fear of mine, being late and getting into trouble. Although I was a lively, talkative child at home, I was compliant at school, always wanting to be liked and to please my teachers.

There was, however, one teacher I could never please: Miss Brown. I was seven and in Junior 1 when I was in her class - and I was terrified of her. She was an old-fashioned teacher, strict, unapproachable and she seemed to like showing children up. Very different to all the other more progressive teachers at William Temple School. She was very hot on grammar, the Bible and maths. Maths - the subject I was hopeless at. A teaching method she used, was to write some sums on the blackboard and get individual children to do the work in chalk on the board. Try as I would, I was often unable to do the sums I was asked to do. I became very worried; I would cry to Mum about it and she decided to go and visit Miss Brown. While Mum was there, Miss Brown seemed understanding and helpful, however, the moment she was gone, Miss Brown told the class that 'a certain girl' was getting upset and crying because she could not do the board work and she named me, "Julie Clappison". Everyone burst out laughing, and then she said how I had to bring my mummy in to ask her to make the sums easier for me. My humiliation was complete. Where maths was concerned, after that, I knew I would always fail.

In Miss Brown's class, Wednesday afternoon was craft class for the girls, which consisted of knitting and sewing: something else I did not excel in. The boys were taken out for woodwork and metalwork. The first thing we had to make was a pale blue knitted potholder. Mine was so poorly made and so full

35

of holes that Miss Brown 'lost' it before I was able to take it home. At least I got Mum's shilling back for the cost of the material. Then, we had to make a small, knitted teddy bear. Mine was yellow with a little red scarf. However, I did not have any kapok to stuff it with (we did not have such things at home). Mum gave me instead an old pyjama jacket of Dad's which she had cut into tiny pieces. Although the teddy itself was not as bad as the potholder had been (certainly, there were less holes), the knitting was still a bit loose and this time one could see the stripey pieces of pyjama jacket showing through. At least, that time, I could blame it on unsuitable materials. I was actually proud of my creation, thinking it was very cute, even though it was not half as good as the ones made by my classmates.

There was one teacher who made the deepest of impressions upon me: Margaret Whitton. She was very young, and I thought she was very beautiful. A truly creative teacher. I loved her, I would have done anything to please her. Just to be in Miss Whitton's class was a joy beyond anything I could ever have imagined. Every day was an adventure with Miss Whitton, she must have worked so hard to make all our lessons so interesting. She told us a lot about her life and was always open to any questions. We had her for two glorious, stimulating and exciting years. During that time, we did lots of creative writing and drama – both my favourite subjects. She read wonderful, amusing books to us, books like The Family from One End Street, Stig of the Dump and Profession Brainstorm. Our classroom was full of colourful wall displays, and I was often tasked with helping her to pin up work, staying behind at breaktimes to do so. We even made cheese – it dripped from the ceiling for days. We planted seeds and watched them grow. We read extracts from Shakespeare and King Arthur's

Round Table, then acted them out. And, best of all, we did a massive scale model of Stonehenge for parents' evening. It was quite breathtaking.

We also took our first school trip to Durham for the day, in a coach, with a packed lunch from home. It was one of the best days of my life. Miss Whitton had studied archaeology at the University of Winchester before becoming a teacher and her enthusiasm for history of all kinds inspired in me a similar interest. Inspirational was what she was. All children should be so fortunate to have such a great teacher.

My school class – I am about 8 years old here (front row, 3rd from right) so it would be Miss Whitton's class.

My hair looks tatty as it was very thick, and I was trying to grow it long. I had a battle with Mum about it's length throughout my childhood. She wanted it short and neat, like Julie Andrews in 'The Sound of Music', and I wanted it long and flowing like Rapunzel. As you can see, Mum usually won!

CHAPTER 5 : Being Ill

I did not always enjoy good health as a child and what happened to me in those far off 1960s days had a deep and detrimental effect on the whole of the rest of my life. Mum made sure we were up to date with our childhood illness jabs, fewer than children have today. When I was around the age of five, Polio became a major health threat within Britain. Mum was not given to fears and fancies, but Polio was something that absolutely terrified her. When a vaccine came out, everyone wanted it for themselves and their families. Mum said she used to wake up in a cold sweat several days on the trot, afraid we would catch Polio before we could have the vaccine. The rough school across the road was doing jabs for children and adults and vaccine on sugar lumps for pre-school children. My mum took Neil in the daytime, but Dad needed to take me in the evening after he got back from work.

It was a freezing cold winter's night when we went to get vaccinated, dark and rainy. The queue for the vaccination was long, it snaked all down the street and round the corner. I stood there in my winter coat, hat and mittens holding Dad's hand. We were there for such a long time and I soon realised that I needed to go to the toilet. "Daddy, I need a wee!", I announced. "Just hold on", Dad said, "we'll be there soon. We'll find you a toilet when we get inside the school." "But I need a wee now, I can't wait", was my reply. Dad said, "Well we can't leave the queue now. If you really can't hold on, you'll just have to wet yourself." So that is what I did. By the time we got to the doctor administering the jab, I was wet, freezing, shivering and, no doubt, also smelling strongly of urine. I cannot imagine that Mum was very happy about that when we got home, but at least I had my protection against the horrors of Polio.

At around the age of three, I started with a hacking cough, and it just would not go. Who knows how it started or where it came from, but I was saddled with this hacking embarrassing cough that wracked my little body. It prevented me from getting a proper night's sleep and it affected my hearing into the bargain. Mum took me up and down to visit our GP on Holderness Road, but my cough refused to go away. In fact, it kept getting worse; it affected everything for me and my family. I tried to stifle it all the time, but it was just no good; it drove us crazy. Eventually, I was referred to the Hull Royal Infirmary for tests on my ears, hearing and chest. I well recall sitting with Mum and baby Neil whilst I sat with a pair of earphones on, and I had to tell different doctors what I could and could not hear. It was quite nice, in a way, having all the attention, but it was also rather frightening as I did not know what was going to happen to me. The hospital seemed huge, grim, dark and old-fashioned. Eventually, a decision was made that was to change my life – something which would make me afraid of medical procedures for the whole of my life.

It was decided that I was to go to stay in hospital for several days to have an operation to take my adenoids out. At that time, I was only five and, in those days, it meant being on my own and separated from my family for a few days on a ward where I knew no one nor what was being done to me. Of course, in our more enlightened times, parents can stay with their children, either on the wards or in nearby accommodation specifically meant for families – not in the 1960s. Children in the 1960s were supposed to just accept that what the doctors were doing would help them. After all, it was only for a few days. I still well remember how terrified I was. I remember my class saying prayers for my speedy recovery before I went in. Mum told me I was going to have my adenoids removed, but I do not remember knowing what they were, and I do not think she knew either, only that the operation would cure my cough.

I remember going on a big blue and white bus with Mum and Neil into the centre of Hull where we met Auntie Fay who was working at Saxone's shoe shop. Mum bought me a pair of slippers as I needed new ones for the hospital - red cord with stencils of animals on them. We also bought a dressing-gown. Then I was booked into the hospital children's ward. Mum and Auntie Fay got me sorted out, putting my few toys and books in a bedside cabinet and helping me to get ready in my pyjamas and dressing-gown. They stayed with me for a little while, but then they had to get back to get Dad's tea ready. I was alone on a huge ward in a high bed, not knowing when I would see my family again. It was one of the bleakest times of my life, certainly the worst experience of my early childhood. I felt so alone, abandoned and let down by those I loved. I was scared and worried about the operation. Would I get any visitors? Would I be in a lot of pain? I longed to be back home, back with my friends at school and playing in the ten foot afterwards. What was going to happen and how long would the ordeal last? I am certain that my future extreme health phobia was created by that horrible early hospital experience. Even now, if I return in my mind to those days, I am thrust back to all those old feelings, fear and anguish. Thankfully, times are more enlightened for children needing hospital care today. At the very least, parents are able to stay with children who have to go through an operation, and they are able to advocate for their children's needs. We did this on many occasions with our own children, especially with Joshua, our eldest.

I do not recall Mum coming to visit at all during my hospital stay. I remember being very quiet and crying a lot. I remember sitting in a little chair with lots of other children watching Top of the Pops on a black and white TV. The number one record at that time was 'Millie' singing *My Boy Lollipop* and we sang along to it. Dad came to visit whilst I was in the TV lounge and I remember not being very happy to see him as I felt so let down, plus I was trying to watch the programme. He later remarked that I had not given him a very warm welcome.

I cannot remember the operation at all (I must have blanked it all out), but I do remember coming round from the general anaesthetic, feeling tired and sick. I was given a meal not long after and I remember some of the children being given ice cream for pudding. When I asked why I had no ice cream, the nurse said the other children had had their tonsils out, so their throats were sore, and they were given food that was easier to swallow. The little boy in the next bed kept coming to chat to me to try to make me smile, but I could not be bothered.

On the Saturday afternoon, we were all given lots of sweets. Now I normally loved sweets and there were all sorts of different ones – a lot more than I would have been given at home – but I was so down, I refused even to touch them. Long after I got home, I used to wish I had eaten all those sweets. It was a measure of how ill and out of sorts I was that I could not bring myself to have them. I let the boy in the next bed eat them eventually. All I wanted was to go home. Finally, after what seemed like weeks, Mum came, and I was discharged from that awful place then we caught the bus back home. That was one of the happiest days of my life.

CHAPTER 6 : Auntie Fay's Wedding

My lovely Auntie Fay told me out in the garden, whilst she was pushing me on the swing, that she had met a handsome soldier from the Royal Marines and that they were going to get married. She showed me a beautiful engagement ring – gold with an opal at the centre which glittered with different colours as it caught the light. I had never seen such an unusual stone. Auntie Fay seemed very happy and excited at the news. I was not sure at all. Would I like this man? He was called Colin, and he would be my Uncle Colin. Would it mean that I would not see Auntie Fay as much after they got married? I loved Auntie Fay and I saw a lot of her. I did not want to lose her to anyone else. Then she asked if I would like to be her littlest bridesmaid. I was five and, to me, being a bridesmaid was probably the most wonderful thing I could expect to happen. Several of my friends at school and on my street had been bridesmaids and I had seen some of the pretty dresses that they had worn and the little jewellery gifts that they had received from the bride for doing their bridesmaid duties. I quickly became almost as excited as Auntie Fay at the prospect of her wedding.

Mrs Jordan – a local dressmaker – had been given the task of making all the dresses for the wedding and, on Saturdays, I went with Auntie Fay and the other bridesmaids for dress fittings. My little dress was fit for a princess with a round neck, puffed sleeves and a sticking out skirt with net layers underneath. We also had to buy frilled ankle socks and white shoes to match the dress. Auntie Fay said I could carry a posy of yellow primroses.

As the great day approached, I got more and more excited, showing off to all who would listen about my important role as Auntie Fay's youngest bridesmaid. As I was often told by Mum, *"Pride goes before a fall"*, and that is exactly what happened on this occasion. A couple of weeks before the wedding, I came down with measles. There was no vaccination for measles when I was little, and it was known to be quite a serious illness. I had to stay in my bedroom and in my bed at first, with the curtains shut to darken the room to protect my eyes. Measles was very bad for the eyes. One of Auntie Fay's work colleagues at the shoe shop had a glass eye because of measles. Mum always reminded me not to stare at it when we went to meet Auntie Fay. Of course, I never obeyed her; that eye used to fascinate me. The doctor prescribed rest, dark and some horrible-tasting pink medicine which made me want to be sick. Dad tried it and he agreed that it did taste awful. Mum brought me my Harold Hare comic, my food on a tray and an eggcup with violets in from the garden. All I wanted to know was: when would the spots go and would I be able to be a bridesmaid at Auntie Fay's wedding? No one would give me any answer beyond "We'll just have to wait and see."

Eventually, it became clear that, although I was recovering, I would not be able to be in the wedding party. I was terribly upset that I would not be the adored littlest bridesmaid, I would not get to wear my princess dress or carry a posy of spring flowers. My disappointment was total. Mum and Dad and Neil would still be going, of course, and, as all of Mum's side of the family were going to be at the wedding, Grandma was going to look after me for the day – just me and Grandma doing all the things I wanted to do at home.

It was one truly wonderful day, one of the golden days of my childhood. What did I want to do, grandma wanted to know. Well, my dolls were my favourite toys, so I decided I wanted to bath them in the washing up bowl as they were all looking a bit grubby. We decided to do this out in the garden, as it was a beautifully sunny day. After they were all bathed and sitting on a towel to dry, we washed all their clothes and hung them out to dry on the washing line. Grandma read me some stories from my favourite Peter Pan book, and we sat and talked afterwards. After all the activity, Grandma decided it was time for us to have some tea. She went to the kitchen to look for some bread to make sandwiches. All she could find was bread suitable to feed to the ducks. So we had ducks' bread for tea and because it was just Grandma and me, we had a laugh about it and enjoyed the best picnic ever, and I basked in all the love and attention of my beloved grandma for the rest of the day. It was almost worth having the measles for.

I did in fact get to wear my bridesmaid's dress. We had a special visit to Beverley Westwood later that summer so Dad could take pictures of me in my dress. Sadly, Mum dyed my white shoes red as she considered them not serviceable as they were. Later on, she also dyed my beloved lemon jeans; she dyed them navy blue. I was upset about them as they were my favourite item of clothing at the time, and I used to mention it occasionally and Mum asked me never to mention it again after she heard me talking about it one time. I think she felt very guilty.

Neil and I looking smart on Beverley Westwood – it
was the only time I got to wear my bridesmaid's dress.

With my beloved Auntie Fay in Nanna and Pop's garden.
Pop loved cultivating flowers after the war, especially roses. He
sometimes used to bring my mum a bunch of sweet peas, which she
loved.

CHAPTER 7 : Teeth

My mum had a very special present for her 21st birthday; she had all her teeth taken out and false ones put in instead. Apparently, this was quite a fashionable thing to do in those days. It meant that you never had to worry again about dental problems or have to go to the dentist on a regular basis. For some people, including my mum, it was a huge relief. After all, who relishes going to the dentist? I horrified my daughter, Francesca's dentist by telling him this story. Of course, by the 1960s, times were slightly more enlightened, and Mum was very concerned about Neil and I and the health of our mouths. This meant regular visits to Dr Lindsay, whose dental surgery was not far from Grandma and Grandad's.

Both Neil and I had a horror of those visits. Dr Lindsay was the least child-friendly dentist – he never spoke to the children he was treating, so it was impossible to know what he was going to do to your teeth. Neil and I seemed to get cavities on a fairly regular basis, and it was frightening to hear the drill and feel the poking and prodding of our mouths as he sought to fill the holes in our teeth. When teeth were really bad, he did extractions using the gas nitrous oxide. I had to be put to sleep a couple of times to have some teeth removed. It was especially frightening as he put a rubber mask over your nose and mouth, and you had to breath in deeply until the gas worked and you were asleep. You woke up with a big gap in your mouth and feeling very groggy. Eventually, I decided that I had had enough of Dr Lindsay and his dental work. Instead of sitting compliantly in the dental chair, I leaped out of it and ran to the front door, beating upon the door and yelling, "Help! Let me out!" My poor mum was mortified and tried to apologise for my embarrassing behaviour. Dr Lindsay's only comment was, "Bring the girl back when she's in a better frame of mind." We never went back there again.

CHAPTER 8 : Holidays

Holidays were very important to our family, especially to Dad. He remembered going to Scarborough for a week's holiday in early September 1939. His parents took him to see a seaside show and one of the comedians was refuting the idea that there might be a war anytime soon. He sang a song which went: "There ain't gonna be no war, no war. There ain't gonna be no war." The audience clapped and cheered in agreement and just the very next day, war with Germany was declared.

Grandad was very risk averse, and he just wanted to get home as quickly as possible now that the war had started. So instead of spending the rest of the week in Scarborough, Grandma, Grandad and my dad hurriedly packed their suitcases and got the next train back to Hull. My dad was deeply disappointed at having to miss most of his summer holiday and he spent the rest of his life ensuring he never had to miss another one.

When I was just three, Mum, Dad, Neil and I were forced to go home from Filey early due to the horrible cough I had developed. It was a windy week and it brought out the worst of that cough. I well remember how upset I felt at the prospect of having to go home and trying to stifle the noise by burying my head in the pillow. However, Mum had made up her mind, so we too had to catch the train home. Only the day before we had been exploring rock pools on Filey Brig and climbing on the side of the cliff, despite me not being very well.

Holidays are high points in everyone's life, something we long for and look forward to, especially when there is not much money about. For a working-class family like ours, holidays had to be saved for throughout the year. To make sure that we children had the most enjoyable of times, Grandma kept a big jar into which she used to put threepenny bits – golden coins with eight sides that looked a little like our present-day pound coins. Just before our holidays, she would take all the money out and give it to Mum and Dad for treats, such as amusement arcades, ice creams, miniature railway rides or boat trips. Mum and Dad also used to give Neil and I eight shillings each to buy ourselves little toys and sweets whilst we were away. This was the only spending money we used to get as the two shillings and sixpence that Dad put in our piggy banks every week was saved up and paid into our Halifax Savings Accounts. It was definitely savings money - not spending money.

Every week, Dad bought us a kids' comic: *Harold Hare* at first for me, later *Treasure*, my favourite and, finally, *Look and Learn*. He used to give us sweets on a Saturday only, although one day I got into terrible trouble for taking more than my amount out of the sweetie jar. Nana and Pop used to visit often at weekends and Nana always brought us a paper bag filled with favourites: penny chocolate bars (would you believe?), liquorice sticks, boxes of sweet cigarettes, foam shrimps and bananas, black jacks, fizzers, love hearts and fruit salads. Nana was always generous with our sweets and we were allowed to eat the whole bag full in one go. Sweets were a huge currency for Neil and I in childhood, but nothing matched the excitement of having real money to spend on holiday.

Holidays for our family meant mostly the North Sea coastal resorts. Days out on the train were always to Bridlington. Filey was our earliest week's holiday, but we progressed to Scarborough as we got older and demanded more in the way of evening entertainment. Dad also wanted to broaden our horizons so one year we went to Bournemouth and another we went to Eastbourne. There was not much to do there, but we did have amazing summer weather that week and spent a lot more time on the beach and had ice cream twice a day. I think it was the first time any of us used suncream, it was so very hot. We actually got to wear our swimsuits (not Mum) on the beach, and it was great to cool off in the sea, but we did not go far in because none of us could swim.

Most of our holidays, however, were far from hot. We got used to sitting on cold, windy beaches and running for cover when it started to rain. One particular Scarborough holiday when I was about nine, it rained hard for most of the week. Despite the fact that we were supposed to be enjoying ourselves, both Neil and I begged for us to stay in the guesthouse to avoid yet another drenching. The problem was that at the genteel guesthouses that we used to go to on holiday, you were supposed to be out of the house after breakfast and you were not supposed to come back again until it was time for the evening meal. Usually, it was all right as most summer weather was warm, even if it was not sunny or fair. That particular week was an almost total washout for us; we spent a lot of time popping into shops and going into amusements. We must have spent a lot of money as well, as we would usually be on the beach paddling and collecting pretty stones and shells and building sandcastles. One day, another guesthouse owner took pity on us as we were so soaked. She let us come in and dry off in the porch. We also went to the cinema one afternoon which took up a couple of hours and at least we were dry, even if the film was not very good.

The problem with guesthouses was the food. Breakfast was usually good, a proper cooked fry-up with fruit juice and cereals, much more than we had at home. Lunch was either a pack-up made in our bedroom by Mum or pastries and cakes bought at the local bakers. We always had a couple of fish and chip lunches eaten inside the chippie. Tea was the unknown meal. Dad was very particular about his food: no tomatoes, no cheese, no herbs and spices, definitely *no* onions or garlic. On of his close friends called him 'the meat and potato pie kid'. The first course was always soup, often tomato, or including onions. We got used to Dad's catchphrase: "What is it, Sylvia?" Dad would not even try anything if it had not been vetted by Mum. The main course could be anything. We had such plain food at home, but many of the things we were given were suspect until Mum had given them 'the ok'. It caused Mum quite a bit of embarrassment and Neil and I a bit of a laugh as she had to reassure Dad that it would not harm him. The pudding course again could be a concern to Dad. We all heaved a sigh of relief it was something like apple pie and custard. Milk pudding or tapioca – "What is it, Sylvia?" My mum certainly had her work cut out with Dad.

A day out in
East Park

North Bay Railway,
Scarborough - a favourite with
our family since it opened in
the 1930s.
A tradition we still enjoy with
our own (now adult) children.

Neil and I playing on our tricycles in the back garden at 28 Beech Avenue.

Waiting for the North Bay Railway train to pass by.

Neil and I on
Filey beach
with
Grandma and
Granddad.

Neil and I with Mum at Swallow Falls,
near Betws-y-Coed in the Welsh
County of Conwy

Neil and I on
Llandudno
beach

**Happy Valley Llandudno.
We loved to picnic there
because the sparrows would
fly down and eat
breadcrumbs from our
hands**

First trip to London. Feeding the pigeons in Trafalgar Square. It was both exciting and slightly terrifying!

Neil and I on Bournemouth beach

Outside Windsor Castle with Neil and Dad. We saw Queen Marys doll's house

Neil and I posing in front of a lovely view of Scarborough Bay and doing the 'Buttercup Test'!

The hottest week's holiday we ever had – Eastbourne (1969?) It was so hot we were allowed 2 lollies a day and we even bought Suncream!

Neil and I with a stunning view of the Hole of Horcum and the North Yorkshire Moors. Mum and Dad loved this scenery.

Many years later we often stopped off here enroute to the North York Moors Railway with our own children

Scarborough beach. We had daily donkey rides, and I always rode on the same one

61

CHAPTER 9 : Birthdays

Birthdays were another highlight of our year. Apart from Christmas, a birthday was the only chance we had of a substantial present, so Neil and I had to consider very carefully what we would like to ask for. As we had no spending money as a general rule, it was something we thought about a lot. Birthdays also meant parties, especially once we began making friends at school, and they carried on until around the age of eight or nine when we were considered too old for them. The very first party I was ever invited to was at the Sally Morell Hairdressing Salon. I believe it was Sally's son's birthday and I was invited because I was around the age of three or four, the same age as him. Mum always had her hair done by Sally as it was just across the road from where we lived, and they were very friendly. Sally did my very first salon haircut and she remarked to my mum that my hair was lovely and thick and that it would eventually perm well. She was right about that. I have photos of myself not long after I started teaching with a hairstyle not unlike that of a toy poodle. It was not a great look, but popular in the 1980s, along with leg warmers and padded shoulders. Anyway, this was my first time at a birthday party. It was at the salon and there was a series of tables down the centre of the room covered with lots of tempting plates of food; a beautiful tablecloth hung almost to the floor. As soon as I realised that Mum intended to drop me off and go back home with baby Neil, I decided I was not going to play any part in the revelries. In fact, I hid underneath the table covered by the tablecloth and nothing anyone said could induce me to come out. Not the prospect of games, prizes, food or sweets. I curled up in a ball and poor Mum had to stay with me, desperately trying, by any means, to coax me out of my hiding place. Nothing worked and we ended up going home. Mum was not happy.

Once I got to school, the party invitations started in earnest. My first was to the sixth birthday party of my classmate, Beverley. I was really excited and hoped I would have a special party dress like most of my friends. Sadly, I had to make do with one of my summer dresses as there were no spare funds for such a luxury item that would only get worn a few times. Parties for children in those days were always thrown at home. There were lots of party games, like: hunt the thimble, run-rabbit-run, musical statues or chairs, memory games, pin the tail on the donkey, and – our highlight – pass the parcel. Pass the parcel packages had a small gift in every layer, so more of the children got sweets and toys. The big prize in the middle was often colouring pencils and a book. Whatever it was, everyone was very competitive and coveted the winning treat, something I was never lucky enough to get, not even at the two parties thrown for me by my own mum and dad!

After a few games, we had tea. The party tea was mainly sandwiches, crisps and orange squash, followed by jelly and ice cream. The pièce de resistance, of course, was the birthday cake, always homemade by the party child's mother and with the requisite number of candles for the child's age. If the birthday cards and presents had not yet been opened, this is when it would happen. After everyone had eaten their cake, there might be a couple more games then all the mums came back to collect their children, who were both tired but also fizzing with excitement (and a sugar rush!), clutching a balloon and, if very lucky, a small party bag with a few sweets and toys in.

After Beverley's party, Mum and Dad decided to throw me one for my sixth birthday. For weeks beforehand, I could hardly contain my excitement. I was going to be the special party girl, showing off to all my friends, winning all the games (hopefully) and receiving lots of presents that I would not usually get. Grandma had even bought me a special plastic tablecloth, pink and covered with pictures of birthday cakes. She also bought me a beautiful doll in a frilly dress. The doll was called 'Belinda' and its main feature of note, apart from the dress, was its waist-length blond hair which could be brushed and combed. Dolls were always my gift of choice until I reached the age of 11, when I was thought to be too old for them by my parents, and I spent so much time brushing and styling Belinda's hair that she rapidly lost a lot of her crowning glory. After a few months, my mum had to give the doll a short, neat haircut, much like my own. I truly loved that doll, but not so much after she lost her hair. Her shortened locks were testament to my over-enthusiasm with the hairbrush.

On the day of my sixth birthday party, I helped Dad to rearrange the living room furniture to make it more party friendly. There was not a lot of room for a large gang of children romping around. I also saw him hiding some pennies around the living and front rooms. When I asked what he was doing, Dad said that each child needed to find a hidden penny to get a balloon. He had a bag full of different shaped and sized balloons, so the sooner a child found a penny, the quicker they could choose the particular balloon that they wanted the most. I had already chosen the balloon that I wanted. It was white with a smiley face and a bright red nose sticking out – it even had a name written on its side,

'Conkey'. So, I made sure I saw where Dad had hidden the pennies so that I could get my balloon. It was cheating, but, after all, it was my party.

The time for the party finally arrived and I began by receiving lots of cards and presents; I was in child heaven, despite my lack of a proper party frock. There were jigsaw puzzles, books (including a beautifully illustrated Bible storybook), boxes of sweets and chocolates, cute soft toys and I was completely overwhelmed by all my party booty. Dad was in charge of all the games and he was very good at organising everything. He needed to take charge quite firmly as we were all very boisterous. Mum, of course, was busy in the kitchen preparing all the party food. Everything went really well, and I was beyond happy. The best ever birthday party. Oh, and I did get my Conkey balloon.

After the tea, Dad decided to slow things down a little. He got all the children to sit down and he read us some stories out of my Bible storybook. I did not hear much of them, however, as I had to go to the toilet to be sick. This was a regular occurrence for me at parties over the next few years. The first time I went to a party when I was not actually sick, I was 13 years old, and it was a sign to me that I was really starting to grow up. The sickness was undoubtedly due to too much food and over excitement, but as a child I was used to being sick as I seemed to have a delicate stomach when young. It did not really trouble me much, but mum hated it because of all the extra washing involved. I well recall notes to school apologising for my absence from classes if I was ill in this way. They always said the same thing: "I am sorry that Julie missed school yesterday, she was bilious." That phrase still makes me smile now; I never heard anyone except mum call it that.

CHAPTER 10 : Autumn Days

Neil and I, as well as several other friends, were very lucky to live in Garden Village, Hull. We lived at 28 Beech Avenue. Our small, square front garden faced onto a road which was always quiet because not very many people had cars in the 1960s. About 50 yards to our left, there was a large grass square surrounded on three sides by shops. There was a chemist shop, where I bought a tiny bottle of perfume for Mum's Mother's Day present. She still had it in her top drawer and I found it after she died. There was Sally Morell's hairdressing salon, the library (where I spent more and more time borrowing books as I grew older), and a general grocer's shop. On the corner, before you got to the chemist, was a white telephone box. No one we knew had a phone at home, it was far too expensive. You only used the telephone box for a real emergency. However, once a year, Dad took us to phone Father Christmas and he would tell us a bedtime story over the phone. The phone box was white, not red, because Hull had its own telephone exchange independent of the national network. My Auntie Nita used to work as a telephonist in Hull city centre, connecting people's calls to one another's phones.

So, we lived in a really pleasant area of Hull. Garden Village had originally been built to house the workers at Reckitts Soap Factory. They made soap powders and the famous 'Reckitts Blue' to whiten one's wash. Mum and Dad were the first of their group of friends to actually buy their own home. A lot of working-class families lived with their parents for a few years after marrying as both buying and renting were expensive, and people married young in those days. Dad's friends thought he was taking a big risk buying property rather than renting at first, but Dad knew he was doing the right thing. Of course, eventually, all his friends also ended up buying their own homes too. My dad was always ambitious and buying a house was an example of that. He could not go to university, but he could and did work his way up the career ladder, changing direction to improve his family's lot. Something his own dad had not been able to do due to a lack of education.

It was the back of our house that was most important for us children. There was a garden where we had a shed and a swing. At the bottom of the garden, we had what we called 'the 10-foot' – a long, wide alleyway separated from the next street by a high fence all the way down – and it was whole lot longer than 10 feet. For us children, it seemed to stretch on for miles and it was our own secluded private playground. It was where we met our friends from the street, where we played skipping games, football, cricket, conkers, races. We played games using our imaginations, pretending to be cowboys or princesses, pirates or spacemen. We rode our scooters, tricycles and bicycles up and down, down the top of Beech Avenue and up to the housing estate at the bottom. We could, and often did, spend all day out there, coming home only when we were called in for dinner or tea. Mum was very glad of that 10-foot; she never worried about us being outside as we were only a short distance away in a car-free secluded playground and it meant she could just get on with all the housework and cooking without us getting under her feet.

From the age of about four onwards, we spent most of our free time outside. It had to be really awful weather for us to be inside the house. Sunny summer days, especially during the seemingly endless school summer holidays, were always our favourite times. However, when summer turned to autumn and we went back to school early in September, Neil and I and our friends started to look forward to the joys of autumn and winter – the biggest highlight of which, of course, was Christmas! Halloween was the first holiday to celebrate. We did not go 'trick or treating', that particular invention did not come over to us from the United States for many years. Instead, our celebrations for Halloween were all conducted through our school. Miss Witton had us make little lanterns out of big potatoes; they had ghoulish faces cut out of the front of the lanterns. The inside of the potato was scraped out and a handle attached to the top so they could be carried home, and inside we put small candles which Miss Witton then lit. The classroom lights were turned off and Miss Witton read us a spine-tingling, horrific story of *Bluebeard.* Bluebeard lived in a huge castle to which he brought his beautiful young new wife. Later he needed to go off on a journey to a far off kingdom and he put her in charge of the castle, tying a huge bunch of keys around her waist so that she could use all the doors, except for a wardrobe in the spare bedroom. The key was there but she was forbidden from opening the door to the wardrobe. Eventually bored and overcome by curiosity, the young bride decided to open the wardrobe. To her horror, the girl discovered that the wardrobe was full of Bluebeard's previous wives, all dead and hanging up in the back of the wardrobe. She was terrified that she might be next and decided she would never admit to disobeying her husband's command. Unfortunately, when she locked the door with the key, she found a spot of blood was staining it and no matter how hard she tried, she could not scrub it clean. I think – I hope – she escaped, but I do not recall the ending. I think it was a happy one for the young bride, and apart from its ending, I never forgot that particular Halloween, so it obviously made a deep impression upon me.

Another time we looked forward to in October was Hull Fair, thought to be the biggest fair in England (although that is disputed by Nottingham with their Goose Fair). It was certainly a massive treat for us children. We always went on the bus just as it was getting dark and the bus was always packed full of people, especially families. The fair was so exciting, but also quite scary. Some of the side shows were far from child-friendly with paintings of ugly witches, half-dressed women and all manner of misshapen animals in jars. One of my favourite side shows was the flea circus where, in a small circus ring on a tabletop, trained fleas could be observed through a magnifying glass as they cycled, boxed or walked on a tightrope. There were stalls where you could get lucky and win a prize. One year, we won two goldfish on 'Hook-a-duck' and had to buy a bowl to go with them. We called our goldfish 'Willy' and 'Jenny' after the children on the TV show called *The Wooden Tops*. One was orange (Willy), Jenny was white with orange markings. Dad (who loved cowboy films) fancied himself as a sharpshooter and he enjoyed trying to win prizes on the shooting range. He did not often win anything but he had fun trying; imagining he was his favourite western actor, 'John Wayne' shooting down cans with a rifle.

My favourite thing at the fair was the helter-skelter. Neil and I used to race to the top of the tower, coconut mats in our hands, and would then slide down the twirly tower, screaming with joy as we went. We used to do this several times on the trot and it was always exhilarating. We used to like to go on the 'cakewalk' as a family. This was a series of moving, shaking walkways and the object of the show was to stay upright and not be jolted off your feet. It really shook you about and made everyone laugh and it was really hard to walk along – you had to cling to the bar at the side. We also loved to visit the 'hall of mirrors', where you saw yourself to be taller, thinner, shorter and fatter and distorted in lots of other different ways. One year, Dad and I went in and, for some reason, could not find our way out again. I found it really distressing as I was only about five and we could see Mum and Neil in the pushchair and Aunty Fay outside, and they could see us, but we just could not get out to them, so what had started as a bit of fun became a real torment. I recall being really scared, crying and banging on the windows in my quest to escape. I think Dad found it all quite amusing; he knew we would get out eventually, but being so young, I thought we might be trapped there forever. It was a huge relief when we finally escaped.

In the middle of the fair was the glittering carousel. It was one of the biggest rides and it was one of the best. The loud organ music that accompanied the ride was an added attraction. There were horses, brightly coloured, with proper leather saddles and harnesses; they had names beautifully painted on their neck. There were also cockerels, sometimes two of them together with a little chariot behind where a couple could sit. It was magnificent to watch as the ride went round in circles, the animals prancing up and down. I longed to go on one of the horses, Mum paid and I clambered on board. As the ride began, my mother warned me, "Don't get off until the ride comes to a complete stop, or you might fall off and get hurt." I remembered and off I went, flying through the cold night air, filled with the scents of hotdogs, toffee apples and candyfloss. I was so happy, it was like being in another world. The ride went faster and faster for ages but gradually it began to slow down and, of course, I waited for it to stop. The trouble was, it did not actually come to a full stop and people were climbing off and climbing on and I could not see my mum, and everything started to blur around me and I could not get off because I had been told not to before it stopped. There I was, trapped, shouting "Mummy!" not knowing what to do and then it started to go again. I had not paid for a second ride, and I was stuck on the horse and I could not see Mum or get off. It was no longer fun - it was terrifying! I then tried to get off and I found myself hanging half on and half off the horse, clinging to its neck for dear life, shouting and crying "Help!" Suddenly, I saw my mum running round the ride after me, trying to catch me before I fell to the ground. She was shouting, telling me to hold on while she tried to get me off that terrifying ride. You might have imagined that would put me off the up and down horses, but it did not. It has always been one of the best rides for me at a fair, and whenever I see one, even now, I just cannot resist a ride on a gilded horse, even at my advanced age!

The highlight of the Autumn – Hull Fair. We got to stay up
late, have lots of rides and visit some side shows.

Neil and I with Dad and the professional photographer's
monkeys. You would be ambushed on your way into the fair,
but for us it was worth it as we loved those moneys!

CHAPTER 11 : Friends and Neighbours

Next door to us, on one side, lived Miss Coltman. She was an elderly spinster lady who we did not see very much. In her garden, right next to our shed, Miss Coltman had a strawberry patch which was of a lot of interest to Neil and I. Sometimes, we were able to reach through the fence and take a couple of strawberries for ourselves. Sometimes, Miss Coltman gave us a small pot of strawberries for our tea.

Next door on the other side lived Mr and Mrs Anderson. They were lovely people, but we only saw Mrs Anderson, who was very friendly with Mum and with me, in particular. Although I had been told by Mum not to bother her, I did often get invited into their house. It used to really embarrass Mum as it was not the 'done thing' to go into anyone else's house unless you were related to them. Mr and Mrs Anderson did not have a proper indoor bathroom. Their bath was under the table in the living room and they must have had a toilet upstairs, but no bathing facilities up there. Mum always said I was not to ask myself over, especially not in the afternoon, as Mr Anderson often had a bath then and the curtains would be firmly shut. The thing I was really interested in at Mrs Anderson's house was the upright piano in the front room. I was occasionally allowed in to have a little play on it. Mrs Anderson would sometimes come in and play a tune, her favourite being *Who Killed Cock Robin.*

Mr and Mrs Anderson had not been able to have their own children, so they had adopted a daughter, Judith, who had grown up, got married and had two young daughters who sometimes made an appearance next door, riding up and down the garden on their tricycles. I did not like them much; I thought they were a bit posh and stand-offish, like Judith (not warm and cosy like Mrs Anderson), and kept well out of their way. I am sure they must have thought I was a right 'Tom-boy' with my short hair, racing round like one of the lads.

Mrs Anderson, like Mum, enjoyed a bit of gardening; in the spring and summer especially, they were outside digging, pruning and planting seeds. Mum told me the names of all the garden flowers. We had lupins, violets, primroses, lily of the valley (my favourites), dahlias, lavender, Michaelmas daisies, iris (that was one of Mum's favourites, as she liked blue flowers) and lots of others. Mrs Anderson showed me how to sow lavender bags to scent clothing drawers with and I recall sunny days sitting sewing on a tartan rug in the garden whilst Mum and Mrs Anderson chatted and got on with the gardening.

Mrs Anderson began to get a little troubled by my lack of a Sunday school education. She was a fervent Christian and she was always at Church on Sundays. She kindly offered to start me at her Church's Sunday school, which took place on Sunday afternoons. Mum was happy about that and I too looked forward to going. Sadly, I only ever went once as I was definitely too much of a handful for Mrs Anderson. Her own adopted daughter had been a very well-behaved child, but I was not like that. I remember that at Sunday school, we all had to sit in a circle on tiny chairs and, of course, I did not know any of the other children there. Mrs Anderson sat with me and it is probably just as well that she did, as I quickly got bored listening to the Bible story. I was, after all, only four and not at school yet. Then there were prayers and, whilst everyone else had their eyes shut, I managed to pinch the cotton handkerchief of the little boy sitting next to me. He started howling because I had his hankie, and the louder he cried, the more I refused to give it back. Not long after the hankie incident, I whispered to Mrs Anderson that I needed to go to the toilet. Mrs Anderson whispered back that I had to wait a bit longer. Unfortunately, I was not able to wait and I left a puddle underneath the chair and another embarrassment for my mother. That was why it was my first and only visit to Sunday school.

Neil and I had a couple of friends down the street with whom we played on the 10-foot. Ann lived about 10 doors down. She was an only child and her mum did not let her out much. I think she thought we were a bit too boisterous for her carefully raised daughter. Ann, in fact, was not a terribly pleasant companion, often trying to get us to do naughty things and then running off to her mother to tell on us.

Next door to Ann lived Mr and Mrs Clayton and their five children. Peter and Olga Clayton were friends of Mum and Dad and they used to go to the same youth group at East Park Baptist Church. They were the first of their set of friends to get married and the only pair to be expecting a baby before they wed – a massive disgrace in the very religious 1950s. It truly was a scandal in those days, but Peter and Olga built a big happy family. Martin was their eldest, then Alan (my age, with a reputation for cheekiness – he once told my mum to "Shut your gums!" when she told him off); next was Roy, then their only daughter, Joan (who was the same age as Neil and my best friend); finally, Ian (a couple of years younger than Joan (thin, weedy, wearing loose fitting shorts that showed his private parts when sitting on the grass, and wearing a pair of the

76

most unflattering round free national health spectacles). We got really fed up with Ian hanging around with us as he seemed so much younger, and Joan was supposed to look after him. He seemed very young for his age and was a real cry-baby. Mrs Anderson was not impressed with the Clayton family one bit. "Why on earth did they go and have all those children when they can't look after any of them properly?" was what she used to say despairingly when one or other of them (generally, Alan) got into mischief.

A few doors away from us, on the other side to the Claytons, lived the Denman family. Mr and Mrs Denman and their two older boys were friends to Neil and me. I used to hang around their garden gate as they had two lovely pets: a tortoise (who was often out on the grass, moving slowly and grazing), and a beautiful old brown dog who used to come up to the gate so that you could stroke his nose. I was always looking out for him as I adored animals. When I was about five years old, the dog stopped coming to the gate. I asked the boys where he was. "You won't see him again," the older one said, "he's gone to the happy hunting ground." I did not know what he meant, so I asked Mum and she gave me my first lesson about death. I was horrified when she told me that it happened to everyone, animals and people alike. "You mustn't worry, though," Mum said, "it only usually happens when people get very old and tired." Somehow, I did not find that at all reassuring. Were not Grandma and Grandad, Nana and Pop old? Surely, that would never happen to them – it must not!

**Neil and I with Grandma and Granddad in their
garden – 63 Lodge Street.**

This was around the time Paul was born

Neil and I in our back garden around the time of Paul's birth

And now with our new baby brother Paul – our family is complete. It's just a pity you can't see his face!

Compared to Neil and I Paul had very few photos taken!

CHAPTER 12 : Our First Pet

The older I became, the louder I clamoured for us to get a pet, a 'proper' one, one with fur. No matter how delightful, I did not consider Willy and Jenny to be real pets because they could not be taken out of their goldfish bowl to be stroked or petted. I wanted a cat most of all, as Grandma had filled me with a huge love for cats. I knew that a dog would be absolutely out of the question due to its need for regular walks, but, surely, a cat would be a lovely pet, furry and companiable, and a cat would be quite independent too – another point in its favour. Of course, I had not reckoned on Mum's strong feelings: very houseproud, she did not want extra work due to the shedding fur of a cat. Also, as a keen gardener, she hated the way that cats would enter the garden and dig up the soil, including the seeds and bulbs that she had planted with care. However, the bottom line was that Mum just did not like cats, despite the fact that, as a child, she had had a cat herself. It was a little black cat called 'Beauty'. Pop brought it home from work; it had been a kitten from a litter produced from a feral cat that used to keep rats and mice at bay. Mum used to dress it up, put it in her dolls pram and take it out for walks. Even the fact that Mum had enjoyed the pleasures of a pet cat herself was not enough to soften her heart towards me having a cat of my own. Whenever I begged for a cat, or even a rabbit, I got the same reply: "You can have as many pets as you like once you have left home, but we aren't going to have one here." And that, I thought, was definitely that.

Dad, however, had a lot of sympathy with my desire for a furry friend and one day, Dad answered my prayers, although my first real furry pet was most definitely not a cat. Dad was always bringing us things home from work on his bicycle. At least once a week, he brought us little treats, there were comics, sweets, stamps for my collection and transfers – our favourites. We used to spend time putting the transfers either in a big book or on our arms. They were a bit like colourful temporary tattoos and to get them to transfer, we had to float them on the top of warm water in a small bowl. It was quite fiddly and, at first, Dad had to do them for us, but as we got a bit older, we were able to do them ourselves.

One evening, however, Dad came home with something much more exciting than even the transfers – he had brought us a pet! We were beside ourselves with excitement; we had no idea this was going to happen. Neither Mum nor Dad had said a word about it, probably in case it did not actually happen. Could it be my much dreamed of kitten? Tied onto the back of his bike with string we could see a cage, so, probably not a kitten. Then Dad went into his saddlebag and got out a small cardboard box. We looked into it eagerly – no pet. Where had it disappeared to? All we could see was an escape hole where the small animal had gnawed its way through. Dad was puzzled and went back to the bike where, at last, he found the small furry golden hamster. It was the sweetest little creature I had ever seen. A wide little body was covered in downy golden-brown fur, a pointed little nose with adorable whiskers at the sides, huge black eyes that gazed into ours and a tiny little stumpy tail, like a grain of white rice. Dad put it on the table and, straight away, it stood up on its hind legs and started to give itself a very thorough wash. We were totally smitten. It was so sweet and it was ready to be held, stroked and loved – the perfect pet for us.

Dad prepared the cage with sawdust and straw, fastened a water pot on the side and a small bowl of dried food for the hamster to eat. 'Hammy' (that was his name) went straight to the food bowl but, much to our amusement, began, not to eat the sunflower seeds and grain flakes, but to push them into the enormous pouches he had in his cheeks. It made us laugh out loud to see how he could store his food for later in his own body. Dad told us that Hammy was an unwanted (how could that be possible?) pet. One of his colleagues at Paragon Station had bought the hamster for his daughter, but she had quickly tired of him, so, on hearing that I longed for an animal to love, he offered him to Dad for me. I adored that little Hammy hamster. Although he was meant to sleep in the daytime, I was forever waking him up and taking him out to stroke or allow him to run around the living room. One day, I saved him from being burnt by the iron Mum and just put onto the floor and as I grabbed him, he bit me and drew blood. Being rodents, hamsters have long, very sharp and efficient teeth. It took me some time to forgive him (at least a couple of hours).

One of my happiest memories of Hammy is of me bouncing him up and down by the window to Cliff Richard's hit song *We're All Going on a Summer Holiday*. I also used to spend hours just watching him in his cage, racing up and down, storing food in his pouches and going compulsively round and round in his wheel, which squeaked as it turned.

Sadly, hamsters do not live very long and Hammy had already spent some time with another family. His death made me grieve for days - we even had a proper funeral. We buried him in the front garden in a *Lyons* sponge cake box. I said prayers and gave a short eulogy about how much we all loved him,

82

and I would never forget him. After the burial, I laid a bunch of lily of the valley on top of the grave and I used to regularly visit him with more flowers.

We had other hamsters after Hammy, they were all named 'Hammy', but he was our first and my favourite.

CHAPTER 13 : We Get a Car

There were not many people in Hull in the 1960s who had a car, not near us in Garden Village anyway; cars were quite a novelty. A man at the top of Beech Avenue had one and sometimes people came to visit friends and family in a car. However, we did not personally know any people who owned a car, apart from Mr Taylor, he was a taxi driver, Mum and Dad said. He was the slowest driver in Hull, and you booked him in an emergency. The only time we booked him was on Christmas Day to take us to Grandma and Grandad's house for Christmas lunch and later to Nana and Pop's for tea, then finally back to 28 Beech Avenue. There was always an air of excitement when we got a lift in Taylor's Taxi.

At the top of the Oval, Neil and I used to marvel at a space age looking car. It was called a 'bubble car' and it was red and round with glass windows revealing the driver inside. We never saw it moving, but we used to think it was the height of sophistication. One day, however, Dad came home with great news – he was going on a course, as part of his job, to learn to drive. If he succeeded and passed the driving test at the end of it, he would be allocated a car for work and he would be able to bring it home to use for us too. This was a real step up for us as a family. No more going on holiday by train, no more heavy shopping bags to strain our arms – Dad could pick us up! And the prospect of days out in the countryside was an exciting one too.

Dad did indeed pass his driving test and he came home in a brand-new navy-blue *Anglia.* It was lunchtime, and after we had all eaten, Dad asked Neil and I if we would like a little run around Garden Village in the car just to try it out. So excited was I to be going in our lovely shiny car with the idea of waving to all my envious friends as I whizzed by, that I did not even put my outdoor shoes on; I went out in my slippers. All was well at first and the car made short work of all the streets near our home. However, as we approached the top of Holderness Road, we needed to brake as another car passed us and a terrible thing happened: the car stalled and then came to a juddering stop. And try as he might, Dad could not get the engine to start again. So there Neil and I were stranded about half a mile from home, a long way from school (which we needed to get back to for the afternoon) and me in my slippers. As I was (and am) wont to do in a crisis, I panicked and started to cry, blaming Dad for taking us for a ride without any idea of how to get us back home, let alone to school. I leapt out of the car and started to run home as fast as I could go, terrified that I would be late for the afternoon classes. I was also worried about what Mum would say when she saw my new ripped slippers. Neil stayed with Dad until the car was fixed, but I was just glad to rush home and get back to school only a few minutes late.

CHAPTER 14 : Leisure Time

Before Mum and Dad had me, they both used to enjoy leisure time activities that were nothing to do with their home and family. Mum's particular love was of reading and with the leftover money from her job as a sales assistant at Hammonds Department Store, she bought books. She told me how, on good weather days, she used to sit in Spring Gardens and read the books she had bought whilst eating her sandwiches at lunchtime. Some of these books passed down to me, she had several of the *Little Women* series (her and my favourite). Mum loved the classics, especially the Bronte sisters, Charles Dickens and Jane Austen. But she also bought new books, such as *Anne Frank's Diary*. Sadly, once I was born, I do not believe Mum ever read another book. Housework and childcare took up all her time and she never went back to reading books again. The most Mum allowed herself to read was *The Daily Mail* and a magazine, such as *Woman's Weekly*.

However, Mum had other, more practical, leisure interests. She was great at sewing and enjoyed making clothes. She told me that when her sisters, Fay and Nita, were little, she not only sewed (by hand) a lot of their dresses, she also made the patterns for the dresses. I do not think she made Neil and I any outfits like that, but when I was 18 and went to America for a few months, she made me a lovely blue and white seersucker sun dress, all by hand, and decorated it with 'bric brac' braid. I loved that dress and wore it for years. It was a practical demonstration of her love for me and a gift to show she would miss me whilst I was away.

Something Mum continued to do for all the family was to knit woollen clothes for us. She had lots of knitting patterns for baby clothes, and she also got some new ones from the magazines she read. Most of our cardigans and jumpers were hand-made by Mum, as well as any hats and gloves we needed. I still have a pair of camel-coloured wool mittens with blue and red stripes she made for me when I left home to go to teacher training college. They are just as warm and hard-wearing now as the day she knitted them. When Neil, Paul and I had our children, Mum knitted clothes for all of them. I think my favourite clothes of all the things Mum knitted, were a set of matinee jackets, dresses and bonnets, and booties in a 'blackberry' stitch. She used that pattern lots of times, it was one she got from Woman's Weekly. By the time my youngest child, Francesca, was born, Mum's hands were deformed due to rheumatoid arthritis. I do not know how she did it, but she managed to knit a tiny bonnet and matinee cardigan for Francesca. It was a true labour of love and probably the last thing she was able to knit. I cherish it now and hope to pass it on to a grandchild of my own one day. One thing is certain – I will not be doing any knitting for my grandchildren. I did used to knit clothes for my dolls under Mum's tutelage, but she never taught me how to cast on and cast off, so I was not able to start or finish knitting without her help.

Dad's leisure interests tended to be more active and outdoors orientated. He loved sport, especially rugby league; he was an avid fan of Hull Kingston Rovers. Even when he moved away from Hull, he often used to travel back to Hull, and to other places, to watch his team play. After his death, Neil, Paul and I paid for a brick in his name to be place in a special memorial wall so he will always be remembered alongside his beloved team. Dad's love of Hull Kinston Rovers took up a lot of his time, especially during the autumn and winter.

As a young man, Dad used to play cricket for East Park Baptist Church cricket team. That took up even more time than rugby and that took place in the summer. He was a very good player, especially as a bowler, and he had a mantelpiece full of silver cups to prove it. Mum, Neil and I very occasionally used to go to watch Dad and the team play on particularly nice sunny Saturdays, but we quickly got bored, and so did Mum, so we elected to stay at home. Dad's desire to play so much cricket became a real bone of contention between them and I well remember a lot of arguments between our parents because of it. Mum resented having to stay at home doing the same domestic chores and looking after Neil and I as on a week day. She wanted a break from the regular routine, perhaps to go out shopping in town, or to East Park.

Both Mum and Dad could be quite fiery and passionate when they rowed, and I well recall Mum occasionally packing a bag and threatening to leave Dad. I have no idea where she would go, perhaps back to Nana and Pop's. Luckily, she never actually made it out of the door. It gave me ideas though, and I too, as a small child, sometimes packed a bag full of toys, clothes and my piggy bank and I headed off down the road after falling out with my parents. They never came after me and I always ended up trudging home on my own, my anger having fizzled out somewhere between Beech Avenue and Holderness Road. I too had inherited their fiery temperaments.

There was one leisure activity that Mum and Dad agreed on and did together. It was something Mum had been introduced to by her parents and which she in turn introduced to Dad: musical theatre. Nana and Pop used to go to the New Theatre in Hull to see the latest musical shows. They also used to go to see the amateur theatre shows. Mum used to go too and I was also taken as a young child to see the Amateur Society shows. The first one I ever saw at the age of five was *Annie Get Your Gun*. I absolutely fell in love with musicals that afternoon and they have been a massive part of my life ever since. Mum had enjoyed some of the more old-fashioned musicals with her parents, they do not do these anymore. Ones such as: *The White Horse Inn*, *Lilac Time*, *The Student Prince*. They were more like operettas than the later musicals that evolved from them.

Amongst Mum and Dad's favourites were all the Rodgers and Hammerstein musicals: *South Pacific* (my favourite), *The Sound of Music*, *Oklahoma!*, *Carousel*. Neil and I once did a reel-to-reel tape of Okalahoma! he sang most of the male parts and I did the female ones. It was great fun. After Mum and Dad died, they left thousands of programmes from all the shows they had seen over the years and it was a great joy, as well as a huge sadness, going through them all, remembering special times when we had been to the theatre together. Mum said she loved going to the theatre as the shows usually lifted her spirits. She was not as keen on the sadder ones, such as *West Side Story*, *Blood Brothers* (I love that one, but it is quite gritty) and she never enjoyed *Fiddler on the Roof.*

Both Mum and Dad loved Andrew Lloyd Webber musicals, especially *Phantom of the Opera*, which was my dad's favourite. They took me to see it for the first time in London to celebrate my 50th birthday and I found it very inspirational. Mum and Dad had seen is umpteen times. Dad's favourite scene was *Masquerade* because all the costumes were so colourful.

Dad naturally passed on his love for both cricket and rugby to both his sons. However, I always hated sport because it reminded me of all the rows Mum and Dad had over Dad's desire to either play or be a spectator. One of Neil's favourite stories is about the first time he ever went to a rugby match with Dad. He and I both had little baskets and, this particular morning, we had a contest to see who could gather the most berries to fill our baskets with. When we got back to our garden, it was clear that Neil had collected more berries than me, which made him the winner of the contest. In a fit of anger, I tipped his basket of berries onto the grass and stamped on them. Neil was dreadfully upset and ran indoors in tears. To calm Neil down and to take him away from me so we did not continue our feud, Dad offered to take him to rugby that afternoon. The die was cast: after that day, Neil always went to rugby with Dad and Hull Kington Rovers became his team just as much as it was Dad's. That continued for the rest of Dad's life and it kept Neil and Dad close as father and son.

Neil and I on a sunny day in front of a floral display in East Park.

You can see from my hair band that I'm having yet another attempt at growing my hair long….

CHAPTER 15 : Bonfire Night

One of the greatest highlights of the autumn term for most children in the 1960s was Bonfire Night. We were taught the story of how Catholic Guy Fawkes and his co-conspirators plotted to blow up Parliament, 'The Gunpowder Plot', as it came to be known. We learned about at school and *Blue Peter* (the children's TV programme) always featured a section of their programme on 5th November to deal with the history of our celebrations, so we were well-prepared. Blue Peter also always led the way with bonfire and firework safety, advising parents to keep fireworks in an old tin and keep children at a suitable distance when setting off fireworks in the garden. We watched all this information avidly, but if we had followed it to the letter, we would not have been able to have our family bonfire night at all.

'Rockets' were always put into old glass milk bottles before Dad lit the blue touch paper and 'retired', as it said on the Standard Fireworks box. And the milk bottles were put on the top of our old wooden step stool (which was about 5 or 6 feet high) before being let off. It was not very 'safety first' conscious and we had one or two 'incidents' over the years. Nothing too bad, just enough to give us a bit of a scary thrill. We loved being outside in the garden with Mum and Dad in the dark – the only night of the year we were allowed to do that. We also told some of the neighbours so that they could join in with us if they wanted, or, if not, at least they were warned that there would be some noises coming from our garden.

One night, Mrs Anderson came outside to see the display, but she left her back door open. Dad lit a small aeroplane shaped firework on the top of the steps. It took off with a whizz and it ended up in Mrs Anderson's kitchen, where it exploded in a cloud of sparks. Mum and Dad were very concerned about the damage it could have done, whilst Neil and I giggled excitedly as they all rushed to put out the little fire that had been caused. Luckly, it exploded into the sink and all was well, but it was an exciting time, and one I will never forget.

'Jumping jacks' were another unpredictable firework. They have, I believe, now been banned due to health and safety concerns. They were put on the floor and lit and they would jump all over the place with the potential to cause burns, but it was okay because Neil and I were always quick to escape from those jumping jacks.

'Roman candles' were static stick-like fireworks from which multi-coloured sparkling starts leapt out of the top. The worst part of them came at the end when several loud bangs announced that the firework had ended. Compared to the blasts of modern-day fireworks, however, these were tame – it was just enough to make you jump a bit.

My favourite fireworks were the 'Catherine wheels' which needed to be hammered onto our wooden fence, then lit. You had to be very lucky to get one that actually worked and went round and round shedding sparks of all different colours, mostly they went round for a half turn and then got stuck on the fence, so they did not tend to be very successful and were usually very disappointing.

Dad loved doing the garden firework displays – he was the perfect showman. He would read all the information to us about the name of each firework and what it was going to do (if all went well). He liked ramping up the excitement with speculation about what might happen if we did not stand well back. It was all such a lot of fun and by far the best night of the year. However, just because Bonfire Night was over, it did not mean the end of our enjoyment. The next day, with the smell of gunpowder still lingering in the air, Neil and I would be given one of Mum's old metal buckets and allowed to go up and down the 10-foot filling it with old spent fireworks, when Neil and I would have our own 'pretend' Bonfire Night ('Bonfire Day') in our garden, which doubled our pleasure. We also spent time doing colourful pictures of all the different fireworks.

CHAPTER 16 : The Most Wonderful Time of the Year

To Neil and I, Christmas was something we looked forward to with eager expectation as soon as we went back to school in September, and it was not just Christmas Day we were looking forward to either. It was the entire Advent season and all the preparations we had to make before the big day itself.

As Archbishop William Temple School was closely entwined with St Columba's Church, there were special Advent services to attend there before the Christmas holidays. Every year we had an end of term Christmas concert, which took place in the evening and was very exciting because all the parents were invited to attend. When I was five years old, our class was all dressed up as elves, fairies and reindeer to sing a selection of Christmas songs and carols. My friend, Michelle Jones, was going to be Rudolph the Red-nosed Reindeer. However, on the night of the concert, her mother said she would not be able to take part as she had been sick on the way home. Miss Taylor, our teacher, looked around for a child who could take her place as Rudolph and – wonder of wonders – I was chosen. What an honour! What huge excitement! I was beside myself with joy. No longer would I be the girl at the back, one of the chorus, I would be Rudolph with a red nose at the head of Father Christmas' sleigh and, at the end of the song, all the other reindeer who "used to laugh and call him names" would be crowding around me, hugging me and congratulating me. For, as the song goes, "Then all the reindeer loved him as they shouted out with glee, 'Rudolph the Red-nosed Reindeer, you'll go down in history!'" I did not even have to sing that bit, the other children were all singing to me and I stood there, beaming with happiness. I knew Mum would be so pleased to see me in my starring role and, to differentiate me from the other *ordinary* reindeer, Miss Taylor used her bright red lipstick to give me the necessary red nose. I will never forget the feeling of standing on the stage in the school hall under the special lights and being part of that production. It awoke in me a desire to be involved in as many plays as I could in the future. Neil too, as he got a little older and started school, began to play his part in the Christmas shows also. There is a delightful photo of him dressed as an elf in a pointed hat for his first school play. I think all the children at school enjoyed that part of preparing for Christmas every year.

Of course, Christmas at school is a lovely time for children – and teachers – I especially enjoyed it myself when I was teaching in primary school. Every classroom had its own Christmas tree onto which we put decorations that we made and there was an especially large tree covered in lights and toys in the school hall. We also made our own hand-made cards as well as taking shop-bought cards that went into the school's special Christmas postal service for our friends. We also always made some little gifts to give to our mums and dads.

One of my favourite TV shows (Blue Peter) always ran a special Christmas charity event for those less fortunate. Sometimes it was for people abroad, sometimes it was for those at home, and Neil and I always got involved. One year, it was collecting foil milk bottle tops which we duly washed and, when we had a large number, sent to the Blue Peter studio. One year, it was used stamps, and, the best year by far, was the year we were encouraged to do a door-to-door sale of unwanted items from home: old toys, books, toiletries, and one I particularly remember (because it never sold), a mustard coloured itchy-looking scarf. Neil and I went from door to door collecting a lot of pennies for Blue Peter and, although it was cold, enjoying every minute.

One house at the top of the street had a sign outside: "Kittens - free to good homes". I told Neil that we would get to see the kittens as well as getting money for the appeal. I lied, dear reader. I told the nice lady who came to the door that as well as selling her some useful items from our box, we would like to come in to see her kittens as our mum said we could have one. I do not know if she believed us, but sure enough, we were allowed into her kitchen where the kittens were in a pet bed with their mother. We spent quite some time stroking the kittens before relieving the woman of her money and then heading back home.

Neil and I were also allowed a little money with which to buy presents for Mum and Dad. Now Dad was a big Shirley Bassey fan and I had just enough money to buy him her latest single; I knew he would love it. I made the mistake of asking Dad if he could guess what I had bought him for Christmas: "Socks." "No." "Mints." (another of his favourite things.) "No." "Chocolates." "No. You'll never guess Daddy." "A book." "No." "One last guess." "A Shirley Bassey record?" My surprise was ruined and I ran to Mum in tears.

All these special events often took place weeks before Christmas Day, but there was one special event every year that Neil and I especially looked forward to and longed for: The Christmas Fayre at East Park Baptist Church. Grandma and Grandad gave Neil and I a few shillings each to spend. We would stay at their house all morning that day and have dinner with them, usually fishcakes, mash and mushy peas. Then we would look at Grandma's finished Christmas cake which she had iced with teeth-breaking royal Icing, flecked up to look like snow and on which she had put plastic snowmen, holly, a Father Christmas with his sleigh and a sign saying "Merry Christmas" in silver. That cake was a wonderful sign to us that it was nearly Christmas Day. After viewing the cake, we waited with growing impatience as Grandma read her Bible, said her prayers, plaited her never-cut hair and twirled it around the back of her head. Then we all had to get our winter coats and hats on and walk down with Grandma and Grandad to the Church.

Inside East Park Baptist Church Hall, all the stalls were set out ready for the customers to come and swell the Church coffers. Every stall was beautifully laid out. There were cake stalls, a dolls' clothes stall (my favourite), a book stall, various games and a 'guess how many Smarties in the jar' stall. There were home-made cards, gift wrap, Christmas tree decorations, a veritable Aladdin's cave of treats and sweets – all so cheap! Cheap enough for us children to buy several items to take home, so long as we were careful totting up the prices. I particularly longed to buy my dolls some clothes, but they were probably the most expensive items I could get, so I bought a few other things first and went back to the doll stall later with my remaining money. The stallholder would sometimes take pity on me and knock a bit off the price if there was an outfit I had set my heart on.

Neil raced around, desperate to spend his cash as quickly as possible on toy cars and bags of sweet wrapped in cellophane. It was like being in Heaven.

Eventually we had spent all our money, and it was time to go back to Grandma and Grandad's in preparation for Dad to come and take us home.

One memorable year, we even won the Smarties in the jar game and were able to take our prize of a box of Dairy Milk Chocolates home to our mum. We were exhausted, elated, but also a little bit sad as it would be another year before the Christmas Fayre came round again.

Many years later, when I was in my mid-twenties, Dad was invited back to East Park Baptist Church as a guest of honour to open the Christmas Fayre. I jumped at the chance to go one more time with my parents. It was just as much fun and just as good value as it had been when I was a child and buying things from the stalls was like going back in time to my childhood. I still have some much faded little pink and yellow umbrella-shaped tree decorations that I put on our family's Christmas tree every year. A happy reminder of one of the best days of the year and my wonderful, much loved and much missed Grandma and Grandad.

CHAPTER 17 : Christmas Day

Every Christmas Eve, Neil and I would get together and make a pact. We made a pact to open our Christmas presents slowly to prolong the pleasure, rather than ripping into the paper and grabbing at the contents. This was a decision that I found easy to keep to; Neil, though, did not. So eager was he to get into his presents that despite all his promises, he never managed to keep them. He was just too excited to wait! It was hardly surprising for us – Christmas Day was the highlight of the year, better than birthdays, holidays or parties. Nothing could possibly compare with the orgy of present-receiving that was our early Christmas morning, and it always was *early* – but not as early as we hoped as Mum would not let us go downstairs until she had laid the coal fire and it had warmed up a bit.

From incredibly early on, Neil and I would both be shouting to Mum and Dad, "Has he been yet?" (meaning Father Christmas.) We did not have a stocking; all the presents were downstairs; most were in two pillowcases – one for me and one for Neil – in the living room. The pillowcases were bulging with colourfully wrapped gifts. Neil, of course, made quick work of his presents: a cornucopia of Matchbox and Dinky cars, footballs, jigsaws, board games, toy trains, selection boxes of chocolates, new clothes and TV annuals. My pillowcases were always full of more girlie items. One year, I got a china doll (Disney's *Cinderella*) with a girl's watch with a pale blue strap to match. Sometimes, I would get doll shoes, clothes and hats, but only one year did I get a doll, as I usually got one from Grandma and Grandad for my birthday, which was only two weeks before Christmas. The year I got a doll for Christmas, I was eight and the doll was very special because it was a baby doll that could take a bottle and then wet its nappy. I adored it and spent the whole day feeding and then changing its terry towelling nappy. I also got annuals, jigsaws and board games, dresses and pyjamas.

Just when we thought things could not get any better, Dad would say, "Father Christmas has left you some special presents." "Where? Where are they?" we would shout. "They're in the front room." Dad would reply. We hardly ever went into the front room, it was for 'best' and too expensive to heat on a regular basis. Mum cleaned it, but that was all. It was used for high days and holidays, which rarely came, but Christmas was one of those special days. These were our 'big' presents and there was one each. It might be something like a tricycle, scooter, doll's house, bicycle, train set, large toys like a racing car track. Things that would not fit in the pillowcases and were difficult to wrap. They were the best toys of the lot and we could not wait to play with them.

After all the excitement, Mum managed to get us to eat a little breakfast which we both bolted down so that we could have as much time with our new toys as possible before we had to leave the house to go to Grandma and Grandad's for Christmas dinner. As we lived a mile or so from Grandma and Grandad's and because it was Christmas, we had ordered Mr Taylor to pick us up in his Taylor's Taxi. For us children, it was wonderful to get a ride in a car. No matter how slow it went (and Mr Taylor was such a slow driver; I doubt we travelled at more than 20 miles an hour), we absolutely loved going to Grandma and Grandad's for Christmas dinner. All the attention was on Neil and I at their house and we got to show them all our favourite new toys. The dinner table was set in Christmas finery and crackers sat at the head of every place setting. It really was a very special meal for us all and even more special because we shared it with such wonderful people who loved us so very much. We never had turkey in those days though, it was chicken or a capon, or rabbit (that was for Grandad as he preferred that), roast potatoes, sprouts (always Dad's favourite vegetables), carrots and peas followed by Christmas pudding with custard or white sauce. No alcohol – Grandma and Grandad were teetotal.

After everything was cleared away and the washing up done, Grandma would take Neil and I into the front room where she had us dress up to distribute her presents to the grown-ups of the family. Neil was Father Christmas in a red cloak and hood and I was a Christmas fairy in a pretty green dress. Grandma even had a hessian sack which we loaded full of presents. We then went into the living room and with Neil giving a jolly "Ho, ho, ho", we proceeded to give out the gifts. They were always the same: everyone got a pair of slippers, there were also men's hankies for Dad and Grandad and embroidered ladies' hankies for Mum. We children had more sweets and chocolates and I cannot recall if Grandma got anything. She may have, but I do not remember it, that was just how she gave out her presents after dinner. We all then crowded round the black and white TV set to watch a very special programme which was on every Christmas Day – 'Disney Time'. The only time in the 1960s that children could see extracts from Disney cartoon films, apart from going to the cinema. Whilst we were watching, Grandma cut her beautiful Christmas cake and we all had a piece with a cup of tea.

Too soon for us children, Taylor's Taxi was back to whisk us off (at a sedate pace, of course) to Nana and Pop's house for Christmas Day tea. I always used to wish we could stay at Grandma and Grandad's, but it was not possible. All the grandparents wanted to see us on such a special day, so off we went waving a sad farewell.

At Grandma and Grandad's, the emphasis was always on us, the children. It was clear at Nana and Pop's that the focus was on the adults. It was a lot less relaxed and less child-orientated; Neil and I were expected to sit quietly at the table and let the grown-ups talk. Tea was a cold salad-type meal, bread was cut up in triangles on a side plate, the main plate contained some lettuce, cucumber, sliced tomatoes, a slice of ham and we could add to that pickles, salad cream and beetroot, which I was not keen on because it stained the rest of the food purple. But by far the worst part of going to tea at Nana and Pop's on Christmas Day was their outside toilet. It was freezing outside and always dark and often slippery if ice was about. I used to hate having to go into the garden to use the toilet. They also had hard toilet paper which was unabsorbent and slippery (Izal I think was the make of it – very old-fashioned). We kids put off going to the toilet for as long as we possibly could.

Mum always insisted on the same early nights for her children at Christmas as at any other time of the year, despite Dad's pleas, and soon it was time for Taylor's Taxi to come and take us all back home after our very busy Christmas Day. It was all over for another year; our only reminder a clutch of lovely new toys to keep us busy for the months ahead.

CHAPTER 18 : Snowy Days

Most children love snowy days and Neil and I were no exception. They were something else to look forward to during the long, cold winter, and we never knew when they were going to happen, but when they did, they were magical! To wake to silent mornings, throw back the curtains and see snowflakes falling like feathers covering all the grass and turning our little back garden into a playground, was a wonderful joy. We could not wait to get outside but not, of course, until we had had breakfast and were bundled up in our thickest winter coats, hats, scarves and mittens. Because we often used to come in on wintry days with what we called 'hot ache' in our hands, Mum even put plastic bags over our mittens and held them on with rubber bands. Mum thought of everything in the constant task of keeping us warm, dry and safe. We eagerly pulled on our wellie boots and then, at last, Mum allowed us to go outside into a snowy wonderland.

We did a bit of snowballing, quickly soaking our exposed faces, before getting on with the all-important task of building our big snowman. We never went sledging – we did not have a sledge; too expensive for the short time it might be used and Mum was wary of us meeting up with the rough children to play in the snow. So, a snowman was our main snow-time occupation. It was a big job for just two of us and it involved a lot of heavy work. We often got our seaside buckets and spades from out of the garden shed to assist with the digging.

First, we had to roll the body into a massive man-shaped heap. Then came the much smaller ball for the head. It was hard work and despite the chill weather we could get up a sweat preparing our sculpture. It took a long time to build our 'man', especially as Neil and I kept taking breaks to have a short warm-up in the kitchen before getting back to work. Finally, though, we managed it – the snowman stood like a big white ghost on the lawn. We gathered twigs to make arms, then had to go to Mum and plead for a woolly hat, mittens and a scarf to decorate him properly. That itchy cashmere mustard coloured scarf that we were not able to sell on our Blue Peter door-to-door sale, came in very handy for our snowmen. Mum let us use an old soft carrot for his nose and we used small pieces of coal from the bottom of the coal bucket to give him eyes and a grinning mouth. We admired him for a while, threw a few more snowballs at one another and then retreated to the house where Mum had prepared a bowl of warm (never hot) water in which we could relieve our hot achy hands. Plastic bags were little defence against the huge amounts of snow we had been using and we needed to get back to normal temperature.

The snowman would last a few days and each day we would go out to see it until finally it began to melt away as the sun came out and the temperature rose. It was great fun while it lasted.

CHAPTER 19 : Bullies

Neil, sadly, was a target for bullies throughout his early childhood. He was quite short as a child, sweet and angelic-looking with big grey eyes and white-blond hair, like our Dad. He was also a gentle boy and that, for some twisted reason, attracted some of the nasty and rough boys. I made it my mission, as his older sister, to protect Neil from the bullies whenever I could, especially in the school playground. There were, however, some bullies I was not able to protect Neil from and they were very troublesome to him and to us as a family.

I remember him coming home crying to Mum about the boy who lived on the next street who had forced him to eat laburnum flowers and pods from a tree near our home. Nothing incensed Mum more than her children being bullied by other children and Neil was such a sweet, adored child, there was no way she was going to let this incident go. After all, we all knew that laburnum pods are poisonous and anything could have happened. Neil and I went off with Mum to the boy's house. There are only a few times that I can remember seeing Mum as angry as on that afternoon. She was consumed with fury. The boy's mother did not stand a chance when she came, unknowing, to the front door. Mum confronted her, holding out some of the laburnum pods she had been able to get out of Neil's mouth. She was shouting like a fishwife, yelling that if there was ever a repetition of the bullying Neil had suffered, she would not come round again, but go straight to the police. The woman was terrified at seeing my mum in such a furious state and made an abject apology before promising to punish the miscreant just as soon as she got hold of him. The encounter was thrilling for us children and as we retreated up the garden path, we heard screams of pain as the boy's mother slapped him and shouted at him and told him never to go near Neil ever again. There was no repeat of the incident; mum had done well.

Bullying is, of course, very common amongst children and both Neil, and later on, myself, were bulled at school. Also, sometimes, the very people tasked with protecting children can be the worst bullies of all and, unfortunately, Neil fell foul of one of these: the music teacher at Archbishop William Temple Church School. I do not remember the man's name now, but I think he was the only male teacher on the staff there and he was not a pleasant man. He was good with music, but not with children. He got angry a lot and shouted, and, to us, he seemed quite a frightening figure. It was hard to imagine a pleasant child like Neil being a source for the music teacher's anger, but on this occasion, he was.

Neil seemed very subdued on the way home from school one afternoon and when I looked closer at him, I could see a livid red mark on his face, just under one of his eyes. When I asked him about it, Neil said that the music teacher had got upset with him about the way he was singing and had hit him across the face. He had been wearing a signet ring and it had left a mark on his cheek. Then Neil started to cry, I think he had been in a state of shock before I had spoken to him. I was truly horrified; physical punishment was a regular means of discipline for most children in the 60s – I was smacked quite a bit by Mum, but less so by Dad. It was thought to be irresponsible *not* to smack kids as it did not teach them to behave and be good children. No one really seemed concerned about the long-term effect; that came a lot later. And even now, the debate for and against physical punishment still continues.

However, children would never be hit in our school, and especially not whacked across the face with one's hand, as Neil had been. Again, Mum hit the roof. Without delay, she got on her coat and within minutes of us getting home, we were heading back to school, her practically dragging us, such was her rush to get to see this wicked teacher. No one outside the family was allowed to harm a hair on her children's heads and especially not Neil, who was such a well-behaved boy, both at home and at school. Mum's fury knew no bounds. We stayed outside the classroom and Mum went in to confront the miscreant, this evil teacher who had not only hit Neil but who had left an actual injury on his face. Nothing was going to stop our Mum sorting him out. The door was firmly shut so we could not hear any conversation and when Mum finally emerged, she seemed far from satisfied. The teacher must have had a job on his hands to calm Mum down, but eventually he had managed it. His side of the story was that the smack across the face had been an accident and he had thought that Neil understood that. He said he had apologised at the time and Neil had seemed to accept it. Mum believed the teacher was lying, trying to worm his way out of what he had done. It was Neil's word against the music teacher's and the teacher was an authority figure with powers of persuasion in his armoury. In the end, Mum just had to walk away; the teacher was not going to back down or take any blame for what had occurred. It was an accident, a misunderstanding. The teacher's word against a seven-year-old boy's. She was never convinced. No one knew Neil like Mum did and she always believed Neil and so did I.

CHAPTER 20 : Naughty Stories

One of my favourite books was 'My Naughty Little Sister' and some of my own children's favourite stories were of me as a child, also being naughty. I said to my Auntie Fay, quite recently, that I had not been a well-behaved child and she corrected me, saying I had actually been quite good most of the time. Well, you can judge for yourselves with the following selection of some of my highlights – or should that be 'lowlights'?

Our front room was out best room, used only for cleaning (how did it ever get dirty?) or for special occasions, which hardly ever came. On the mantlepiece was a small collection of ornaments which I, as a small child, was forbidden to touch. One of the ornaments was a china 'Bambi'-style deer (it was given away free with the drink 'Babycham'). It stood in pride of place in the centre of the mantlepiece. It held an irresistible attraction for me and, as a pre-school child, if Mum was busy in the kitchen, I would often sneak off to the front room to play with the Bambi. One day, unfortunately, it slipped out of my hand and fell with a crash onto the ornamental hearth below. It was smashed into several pieces. I was truly shocked and had no idea what to do. I decided to conceal my crime, hoping that Mum would never find the pieces hidden behind one of the cushions on the sofa, and returned to Mum in the kitchen. I must have had a guilty look about me (I have always found it hard to hide my feelings). "What have you been up to?" Mum wanted to know, "Have you been in the front room again?" "No", I replied, horrified that she had guessed that I had something to hide. Mum let me off, then later in the week when she was cleaning the front room, she went to plump up the cushions and, of course, she then found the pieces of the Bambi ornament. I burst into tears when she showed me the pieces and tearfully admitted that yes, it was me who had broken it. I do not recall the punishment (probably a good telling-off). I think the fact that I had broken my favourite ornament was probably punishment enough.

We had a lovely set of studio-style photos of Neil at about the age of six months and me as a nearly three-year old. They were not actually taken in a photographer's studio, they were done in our home (in our front room in fact) by a friend of Dad's. He was a policeman, but he took photos as a hobby. Dad arranged for him to visit one afternoon to take some good quality shots, which were also probably given to our grandparents as Christmas presents. Mum and Dad kept quite a few and they are my favourite photos of Neil and I as children. Dad said to me, before his friend arrived, that the photographer was a policeman, so I was not to call him 'a fair cop' – as if a child so young would ever say that. Of course, I think Dad actually wanted me to say that and me, being a precocious child, was happy to oblige. The moment the man stepped over our doorstep, I asked, "Are you a fair cop?" It was great, because everyone laughed and the attention was back on me for a while instead of on baby Neil, where it usually was in those days. Everyone loves a baby and I was no longer one.

My Dad had not told me how long-winded and tedious the photo session would be. It was all right to start with as the photographer took several good shots of Neil and me together. We both looked like little angels – Neil in his pure white all-in-one romper suit and booties and me in my crisp cotton royal blue and white dress. However, after a while, my interest in the photographer and his camera began to wane, especially as he decided to take some photos of

Neil on a blanket on his own. That was really boring, and my lovely Daddy was far more interested in talking to his policeman friend than he was in talking to me. I wondered how I could get the attention back on myself again. Then it struck me – Dad had told me not to go near, and certainly not to touch the large lamp the photographer had erected for better lighting effects. He said that it would burn me as the bulb was hot. So, I walked straight up to the lamp and put my hand on it. Dad was correct, it was very hot and my hand really hurt where it had burned it. Of course, this occasioned all sorts of fuss. Mum scolding Dad for not keeping an eye on me, me crying in anguish at the pain and having my hand thrust under the cold water tap to take away the sting, and the photography session being held up for several minutes whilst my parents tried to calm me down. At last, peace reigned once more and although my hand stung for quite a while afterwards, at least I got to sit on Dad's knee for a while.

The photographer progressed to a set of photos of all four of us as a family. Sadly, the pain I suffered can be clearly seen in my facial expressions on the final few photos. I look just like a girl who has disobeyed her parents and got herself burnt. I could have saved myself a lot of pain and heartache that day, and many other days, if I had only obeyed the old adage: "Always listen to your parents."

As children, Neil and I, like lots of siblings, had a love/hate relationship. Rivals for Mum and Dad's attention, we often ended up arguing, even physically fighting each other. Neil used to punch me and I used to pinch him. We fell out a lot; it used to drive our poor mum mad. As an only child until the age of 10 herself, she had not suffered the rough and tumble of near-age brothers or sisters, neither had Dad, being an only one. We were a revelation in the depth of our feelings towards one another.

One day, we had the dolls' china tea set out on a cloth in the living room. The idea was that we were having a doll and teddy's tea party whilst Mum went upstairs to clean the bedrooms. It was too cold to play outside, and Mum thought that this would keep us occupied while she was busy. The china tea set was an old toy of Mum's (one of the few) and it is rather lovely – I have it now upstairs in the loft for my own (hopeful) grandchildren to use – well, *most* of it is there anyway. It is white with decorations of pink and grey flowers. There are cups and saucers, a milk jug and a sugar bowl. Not the teapot though. Mum had put some water in the teapot for us to use as pretend tea and Neil and I were both excited about it as it added some interest to our tea party. However, not long after Mum had disappeared upstairs, *Hoover* in hand, we started to disagree about whose turn it was to pour the tea. The disagreement soon turned into a massive standup row with Neil putting his hand on the spout of the teapot and me pulling hard on the handle. We shouted and screamed at one another so loudly that Mum could hear us even over the noise of the vacuum cleaner. She came rushing downstairs to break up the fight but, sadly, she was too late. One enormous final pull had me flying backwards into the wall, teapot in hand, which then smashed against the wall and broke into little pieces. Mum was furious – that was her precious childhood tea set and now the main part of it was broken. Both Neil and I started crying when we saw the damage, knowing the tea set would never be the same after our fight. And it was not. I do not think we played with it much after that, as the teapot was such a vital part of its charm. I think, before it is used again, I will have to source a new teapot for it on 'E-bay'.

As a small child, I had quite a temper. If something went wrong, I let people know about it. I remember coming downstairs early one morning (I must have been only two or, at most, three), angry because I had wet the bed in the night. My pink flannelette pyjamas were soaking wet and the trousers were sticking to my legs. Mum had been laying the fire and, because it was so early, she had not put the fireguard round it as she did not think Neil or I would be out of bed. In a fit of temper, I pulled off my pyjama trousers and threw them angrily into the fire. Up they went in a blaze of flame. Mum came through from the kitchen and I expected to get a smack or a telling off after this act of destruction. Surprisingly, Mum was quite sympathetic at what had happened and she ran a bowl of water to get me thoroughly washed off. The pyjama trousers were beyond salvaging, however.

As a small child, I could be a bit of a 'snitch', especially where Neil was concerned. Sibling rivalry was a very strong force between us and as we got older, it appeared to me that I was a naughty child, and Neil was a good one. So, any reason to get Neil into trouble seemed like a great idea to me. For once, I could polish *my* halo instead of Neil. Both Neil and I loved to hear the bells of the ice cream van. We begged Mum to "stop him and buy one" (as the advert said), but the ice creams were quite expensive, so we were usually refused. Mum said that we were not to go round the house to the front road at any time, and especially not because of *Mr Whippy* as we would not be given money to buy ourselves an ice cream or lolly, so there would be no point in going anyway. She was very concerned about the minimal dangers of the road, so we had a total ban against it. We had to stay and play in the garden and on the 10-foot.

At the time of this particular incident, Neil was just three and I was five. He had a little red three-wheeled tricycle and could get up quite a speed on it. It was a hot, sunny day – perfect for eating ice cream – when we suddenly heard the familiar tune of *Greensleeves* in the air. The ice cream van was coming! Neil straight away got on his trike and peddled as fast as his little legs could carry him. He rode right out of the 10-foot and onto Beech Avenue – he was on a mission to get himself a lolly. I was alerted to what Neil had done by one of the other children we were playing with. I rushed through the house to the front room where I saw a thrilling sight: Neil waiting by the ice cream van. Within a few moments, a lady from further along the road saw Neil waiting and asked him if he would like a lolly. Of course, he said "Yes", and to my excitement, I saw him accept a bright green lollipop from the hand of this stranger. He started to lick it happily; I am sure he said thank you to the lady as he was a polite little boy. I ran to Mum, it was time for me to act. "Mummy, Neil has got on his bike onto the road, right round to the ice cream van and a lady there got him a lolly!" Mum was furious. Not only had Neil ignored her rule about not going round to the front of the house onto the road, he had also accepted a lolly from a stranger! This was a double transgression. I had no idea how Mum would punish this massive infringement of the rules, but I knew it would be something big – and it was. Puce with anger, Mum raced out of the front door, she dragged Neil and his tricycle inside the house where she shouted at him, smacked his bottom and wrenched the lolly out of his hand. Neil started to cry. At this point, I started to feel a little bit sorry for him; I almost wished I had kept the news to myself. However, worse was to come. Mum took the offending lolly into the kitchen; she turned on the tap and to both Neil's and my horror she thrust the lolly into the sink and turned the water full on. The lolly quickly started to melt, "And let that be a lesson to you never to disobey me again!" she yelled. We were both completely stunned by what had happened. I was so shocked and, by now, was feeling really sorry for Neil and really guilty at telling on him. One thing was certain: no matter how hot the day, neither Neil nor I ever transgressed in that way again.

My final naughty story is to do with a school friend's birthday party. I think it was Hazel McDonald's seventh, or maybe eighth birthday, and it was held outside in the summer. Mum had gone out shopping for a card and present whilst I was at school and she had come back with the sweetest little pottery deer with a stuck-on white furry tail. It looked a lot like Bambi and you know that I like those sort of things. I fell in love with it and refused, point blank, to take it as my birthday gift to Hazel. I kicked up quite a fuss and despite Mum's entreaties, I refused to budge. I wanted to keep that toy and so, in the end, Mum had to wrap up one of my unused jigsaw puzzles. It was nice, but not as nice as the toy deer. That said, Hazel was none the wiser and I got to keep the coveted toy. It was a great party, so warm and sunny, we spent a lot of time outdoors playing on her swing and her big slide. No one else had one of those in their garden. Golden days and childhood memories – how quickly they go by.

CHAPTER 21 : The Best News of All

One dinner time, Mum and Dad said they had some good news to tell Neil and I before we went back to school for the afternoon. That news turned out to be life-changing for all of us. It was the best news I could ever have hoped for. Mum and Dad were going to have another baby! A brother or sister for us. Neil seemed a bit shocked, stunned perhaps. It turned out that he was not the only one. Mum told me much later when I was an adult that they had not planned on another baby and, with me aged 10 and Neil eight when the baby would arrive, she had thought that her baby days were in the past. She thought that people might think they were being irresponsible in having a new baby and she herself thought she was a bit too old to have another little one. She said she worried that she would be the oldest mother at the school gates at 33 and the child would be bullied because of it. Like a lot of parents, she had concluded that two children were enough to provide for and worry about, especially as she already had the perfect family: a girl and a boy. However, there was no arguing with nature. The child was on its way. They had kept the news from us children for as long as possible in case of anything going wrong, but the birth was only a few months away now and they thought that relatives might let slip the news if they did not tell us soon.

Despite Mum's many concerns, her attitude to life was that whatever happened, you just had to 'get on with it' – one of her favourite expressions. If it could not be changed, just get on with it; it was no good worrying or moaning. And through the years, Mum's greatest contempt would be reserved for those women who would not just 'get on with it' – women who had abortions. I well remember her saying how little she thought of the female tennis player, Billie Jean King, who had had a termination of a surprise pregnancy. Mum was also full of contempt for women who worked full-time. She called them 'career women' and she almost spat the words out of her mouth as she said them. She said that she and Mrs Anderson (her next-door-neighbour) both concluded that mothers should be at home for their children and how terrible it was for some poor 'latch-key' kids, home alone. Mum would never have left us alone to pursue a job or a career. She saw her role in life as being a full-time housewife and mother as support for Dad, running the home, cooking nourishing meals from scratch, keeping the house spotless and tidy, doing the shopping (an almost daily task as few in the 1960s had freezers), taking the children to and from school and to all their medical appointments. It was truly a full-time job for most women in those days. Mum also did most of the gardening which she saw as a leisure activity, and she knitted quite a large proportion of our clothes. It was all hard work, but I think she enjoyed it most of the time.

Dad always used to say that he was the lord of all outdoor doings and Mum was the lady of all indoor doings, and that was how they lived for the whole of their lives. Anything domestic was Mum's responsibility; anything outside of the house, including paying bills and keeping the accounts as well as full-time paid work, was Dad's responsibility. The world moved on relentlessly, however, with women coming out of the house more and more, but Mum and Dad never moved on with it and I, as an adult, have followed in my Mum's footsteps too. I have always put my home and my family ahead of anything else, which is very old-fashioned, but fortunately, Andrew and I are happy with the arrangement. It has helped us that, like Mum, I am not the slightest bit materialistic and have never been concerned about new clothes, new furnishings, or expensive holidays. I have always enjoyed looking after the children and making sure they had what they needed, if not what they wanted.

I did not marry Andrew until I was around 30 and, due to some ill-health in my 20s, I had been informed that I would not be able to have children without medical intervention, probably IVF. I was absolutely devastated at the news as I had set my heart on getting married and having a larger-than-average family. I knew I would not be able to go through medical procedures to have a family due to my hospital phobia, so had resigned myself to a lifetime of childlessness. However, as a committed Christian, I put my faith in God and the power of prayer and quickly I had four amazing children who are, with Andrew, the centre of my life. They give my life meaning and focus, in a way nothing else could have done. Thanks be to God, and to Mum's example.

My Mum was in a very different situation. She always said, "As soon as your dad puts his slippers by the bed, I am expecting a baby." She never used the term 'pregnant' – she hated that word. And so, in 1967, she found herself expecting an unexpected baby. Dad was absolutely thrilled at the news. He always said the favourite years of his life were when we children were young and we could play with him. He loved taking us for days out and especially on holiday. He was like a big kid himself and once his working day and week were done, gave himself totally up to family life. He was always outside on summer evenings playing cricket up and down the 10-foot with us and other neighbourhood kids. We were so very blessed in having such a devoted dad, as well as a full-time mum. Full-time mums were the norm at that time, but involved dads were quite rare. Dad did not do any practical childcare though, he did not give feeds, or change nappies, although he was always happy to push a pram! No, he did all the fun, entertaining things and Mum too benefitted as she got a bit of free time to just get on or go out shopping.

The more I see of family life these days, the happier I am that I had an old-fashioned traditional family life as a child and Mum and Dad's care continued throughout our adult lives, which is why I miss them so much every single day, even though I am now over 60 myself. No one loved me and my family like they did, and I will be forever grateful for all their love and support. I miss my almost daily long phone calls and the catch-up meals half-way between their house and ours. To have such devoted parents brings a confidence and stability to children's lives that nothing else ever could. They were our ordinary heroes who always put our welfare above their own and I have tried to do the same for my own much-loved children. Mum and Dad definitely led the way.

That long ago dinner time when I learned that we were to have a new sibling, I was over the moon. To me, it was the most exciting news ever. I did not know anyone at school who had a baby brother or sister, and I could hardly wait to get back to school to tell all my friends. I knew I would be the envy of the classroom. It was as if all my dreams had come true.

Now dolls were my favourite toys – I had at least 10 of them – and I spent most of my free time playing with them. But now, I was going to have a real live baby to play with, not just a doll! I would be able to give feeds, bathe, dress and walk the baby in its pram. What more could I possibly want in my young life? I so hoped it would be a girl as I already had a brother, and all my dolls were girls. I particularly liked the idea of dressing up a little girl in frilly dresses, just like I did my favourite baby dolls. I immediately suggested that the new baby might be called by my favourite name at that time: Andrea. I did not have a doll of that name; I had Charlotte, Dinah (I owned a black doll – very unusual at the time), Jenny and Annabel. And I had one doll who looked like either a girl or a boy, so sometimes I called it 'Rose' and sometimes I called it 'Peter'. I did not choose a name for a boy, so certain was I that I was having a little sister. Mum and Dad said they would keep the name 'Andrea' in mind if the child was a girl.

CHAPTER 22 : The Baby is Born

Our six-week school summer holiday started with no sign of the new baby. Every day, I woke up excited, wondering if this would be the day that I would get my baby sister. We broke up in July and still, by early August, no baby had arrived. Meanwhile, my lovely Auntie Fay and Uncle Colin had welcomed their first child into their family. Baby Karen was a delight, a beautiful dark-haired little girl, and Auntie Fay was so happy to be a mum. Mum, Neil and I visited the baby linen shop at the top of the street and bought a pretty little multi-layered dress; it was white and eau de nil (a sort of peppermint green). However, we had to take it back to the shop to exchange it for the same style in all white as Auntie Fay had decided to dress Karen completely in white for the first few months.

Auntie Fay was, of course, a wonderful mother to her new baby and I could not wait for us to have our turn. And then, one night, suddenly, it began to happen. We had been put to bed as usual but after a few hours, Dad came to wake us up. The baby was on its way. Mum and Dad had been watching a western film on TV when Mum realised she would soon be giving birth. Neil and I got dressed as fast as possible. Dad put Mum's hospital bag in the car, then got Mum in the front seat and us in the back and off he drove, faster than normal. In fact, Dad was in such a state of excitement and tension in his rush to get to the maternity hospital, that he ended up missing the turning he needed to take! Neil and I thought it was all really funny, but I do not think that Mum felt the same.

When we finally got to the maternity hospital, we were left in the car whilst Dad took Mum inside and got her booked in and settled. Neil and I were both feeling really tired and Neil said he needed a wee. At first, I told him he would have to wait until Dad got back and we could drive back home, but his need became more pressing the longer we were in the car. We were parked in front of a bush and I suggested he get out and use the bush as a toilet. Neil was pleased as well as relieved to be able to do so. Not long after that, I also felt the urge to go to the toilet and after checking there was no one about, I followed him and did the same. We seemed to be in the car a very long time and we both became very sleepy. As the car was an Anglia with a leaning back shelf, Neil lay down on it and soon fell asleep. As the eldest child, I thought I should stay awake to keep a look out for Dad, or in case anything was to go wrong. Eventually, Dad came back to us and Neil climbed down off the back shelf and we were all able to go back home and to go to bed. Although we were very excited, we were also very exhausted and we were able to get at least a part of a night's sleep.

Very early in the morning, Dad woke us up to tell us he was going to pop across the road to the telephone box to phone the maternity hospital to check if Mum was all right and whether the baby had been born. Neil and I were so incredibly excited, we shot out of bed and got dressed. Within minutes, Dad was back, "Mum's had the baby – it's a boy!", he said. For just a couple of seconds, I felt a little disappointed. I had not really considered that the baby might be a boy, so sure was I that I was having a baby sister. But then, the joy at being a big sister of a baby boy hit me, and it was as if a brother had been what I had wanted all along. "What's the baby's name?" we both wanted to know. "Mum chose the name 'Paul'. The film we were watching last night had a cowboy in it called Paul and we both liked the name" Dad answered. "How is Mum?" was our next question. "She's very tired. The baby's shoulders got stuck and it took a while to free them. But everything is all right now and your Mum is resting."

Paul was Mum's third child and she had not had shoulder dystocia with either myself or Neil. Strangely enough, my third child (Elizabeth) had the same condition, and it was only Andrew shouting loudly at me to push with all my might, as the midwife panicked trying to get a doctor, that saw her delivered safely and without damage to her arms. Up to the point of delivery of the baby shoulders, all had gone well. However, I later learned that shoulder dystocia can cause problems with the baby's shoulders and arms. Fortunately, for both Paul and, later, Elizabeth, they were born without those problems.

Neil and I were beyond excited. All we wanted to do was to go down the street announcing that Paul had been born, and that was what we did. We went around at the same time as the milkman, knocking on our neighbours' doors and announcing the great news of our brother's safe arrival. Everyone we met was so pleased for us, from Mrs Anderson to the Denman family, from the Claytons to Miss Coleman. We knocked on as many doors as we could, sharing our excitement as we went. After we had finished telling the entire street, Dad got us to pack up a few clothes and toys, get into the car and he took us to stay, as planned, at Grandma and Grandad's. He was going into work as, in those days, men did not have paternity leave (men were expected to go straight back to work), although he would visit Mum and the new baby straight after the day's work.

Grandma and Grandad shared our joy at having a new grandchild and were just as excited as us. We knew that Mum and baby Paul were to stay in the maternity hospital for several days and we were very happy to be with Grandma and Grandad, rather than at home. Grandma and Grandad doted on us and were willing and ready to indulge us in any way we wanted. For me, that meant getting Grandma to help me make a whole new set of clothing for my largest walking doll. I especially wanted to make a frilly best dress for her and Grandma had already been shopping to get suitable materials for it. For Neil, it meant a lot of exploring and running about in Grandma and Grandad's large garden.

Dad bought us a gift from the new baby; it was a set of plastic golf clubs and balls and pretend holes and Neil and I had a lot of fun together with that. All seemed to be going well until Dad came back after visiting Mum and baby Paul at the maternity hospital. There were hushed conversations with Grandma and Grandad and when they came back into the living room, we noticed that Grandma was crying. She went straight to her Bible and started to pray. Dad looked very grim; we had never seen him like that before, so we knew something worrying must be happening. Dad told us that baby Paul was very seriously ill. He had been born with a very difficult to sort out condition. He had something called 'imperforate anus', a rare condition which meant he had no back passage or anus. Only a difficult and delicate operation would be enough to save his life. The decision had been made to transfer Paul immediately from the maternity hospital to Hull Royal Infirmary. Neil and I were terribly upset and it was made even worse because we had seen Grandma's reaction. Dad was due to go back, first to visit Mum, then on to Hull Royal to speak to the doctors to see if they could do anything to help Paul. Whatever needed to happen, it needed to happen quickly as the baby would not be able to feed because he would not be able to expel any waste matter from the feeds. Paul's life literally hung in the balance.

As the operation was so rare, there were only two surgeons in the world who were able to do it at that time. As it turned out, one of those surgeons was actually in Hull doing a series of lectures about his work. He had flown in from India. He agreed to do the surgery the very next day. Paul was one day old. Nobody had any idea if the procedure would be a success and, if it were initially successful, Paul would need a lot more treatments in the early years of his life. It was all most dreadfully worrying. Looking back, I do not think anyone expected Paul to pull through. A tiny baby needing major surgery for a condition none of us had ever heard of. It seemed unlikely. Grandma continued to cry and pray and we just hoped for the best.

The atmosphere at Grandma's house was now totally changed. In the space of a few minutes, we went from being full of excitement and joy to worry and fear. Neil and I were just so glad we were able to be cared for by our wonderful grandparents who always put us and our needs first.

The next day, which was 13th August, was the day of Paul's operation and we could not concentrate to play or do anything. It was then that Grandad decided to suggest we do something useful which, if we could do that, would distract Neil and I from our misery and sense of foreboding. "I know what we will do", he said, "I will take you down the road to the bank and they will open a savings account for each of you so Grandma and I can save a bit of money for your future." Neil and I had never been present when Dad opened our Halifax accounts so we had no idea what was involved and we were really pleased about this. Dad was pleased too; he thought we would be busy doing something whilst the operation was taking place, so he would not have to worry about us. Also, it would give Grandma some time and space to pray and to read her Bible, which strengthened her so much.

So, off Neil and I went walking together down to the bank on a lovely summer's day – a day that would change our family's life forever one way or another. Grandad held our hands tightly sharing his knowledge of the world as we walked along. He told us how a rainbow came about, how to tell what the different cloud formations meant, what the different trees we passed were named, we thought he knew so much about the world we lived in, and much of it was self-taught from reading books from the library, watching TV and reading newspapers and the Readers Digest. Although he had hated school, Grandad had a thirst for knowledge which he pursued for the rest of this life, and we thought he was the wisest man we knew.

At the bank, we had to give proof of our identity, had to pay in a bit of money each – Grandad gave us half a crown (two shillings and sixpence or 12½ P) each to open our accounts. And then we had to put our signatures on the bottom of a lot of questions. Neither Neil nor I had ever had to write our signatures before so we spent a bit of time practising how we would do them. It certainly all took our minds off baby Paul's operation. To complete the process, both Neil and I were given a little savings book. When we opened it, our names and addresses were there plus it said we had two shillings and sixpence in our accounts. We felt so rich and important now that we were clients of the bank.

We had been quite a long time at the bank, so we had to hurry back to Grandma as it was nearly time for dinner, which was the main meal of the day at 12.30 every day on the dot. Grandad made us hurry even more when it started to rain – a summer shower unexpectedly – and we had gone out without raincoats or umbrellas. Luckily, the rain did not come to much so we did not get soaked, just a little damp. It was just as well as Grandma would not have been impressed at Grandad's lack of preparedness. We excitedly showed her our brand-new bank books and the money that we already had in our account, and she was suitably impressed.

The rest of that day, however, seemed to drag on and on as we awaited news from Dad. All of a sudden, Dad was back bringing good news. Paul had come through his operation; all had gone well. He would need to be kept in the hospital for several weeks though whilst his condition was monitored, but Paul was definitely through the worst for now. We were all so thrilled to hear that the baby was going to be well and that one day, in the not-too-distant future, he would be able to be brought home to part of our family. How we rejoiced that evening! Grandma cried again – happy tears this time – and went back to her prayers, prayers of gratitude and thanksgiving. We would now be a family of five; better days were on their way.

CHAPTER 23 : Baby Paul Comes Home at Last

Paul had to stay in hospital for several weeks and during that time only Mum and Dad were allowed to visit the special care baby unit. Every time they went, I begged to be able to go and see our little brother; we had not seen so much as a photo. People did not have camera phones or even instamatic cameras in those days. We had a new baby in the family but we were forbidden from seeing him. I was terribly upset about it. Despite my begging, we could not see him.

One weekend, Dad came with great news: he said the matron had agreed to Neil and I going in the see baby Paul at a quiet time on a Sunday afternoon. We could only stay for a few minutes as children were not really allowed in, but the matron made an exception as we were older than the usual siblings who might be expected to visit and Dad had said we would be really quiet and well-behaved. Of course, we would! I would have done anything to see the new baby and felt I had missed such a lot of time with him already.

When we got to the hospital, we had to wait until we got the 'all clear' from matron. The Hull Royal Infirmary was a big new hospital with many floors, so we travelled up to the top floor in a shiny bright lift, it was very high up and we had never been there before. Finally, we were allowed to go in to see baby Paul. The baby was right in the middle of a massive room in a very tiny clear-sided cot. There was no other baby in the room, just Paul. I walked over to the cot, he looked so tiny and was naked, except for a little terry nappy. There were tubes and wires stuck onto his body and machines whirring in the background. It was a wonderful thing to see him, he was the most beautiful baby I had ever seen, and I had seen quite a few when we went shopping with Mum on Holderness Road. I used to spend a lot of time looking in the coach built prams at all the babies left outside the shops.

Paul had white-blond hair like Dad, big eyes, a tiny button nose and a rosebud mouth. I fell totally in love at first sight. I could not take my eyes off him; he was gorgeous and he was all ours. All I wanted to know was when we could take him home and have him all to ourselves. I could not wait to put him in our big navy Silver Cross pram and take him around the streets for a walk, showing him off as I went. Neil, on the other hand, had been displaced by this new younger upstart and I knew the feeling all too well. He did not seem terribly interested in his new brother. He took a quick glance then raced over to the big plate glass windows where he gazed excitedly at the whole panorama laid out before him. Dad joined him and pointed out Hull Kingston Rovers Ground, Craven Park, Grandma and Grandad's house, East Park Baptist Church and the park behind, and lots of other places of note. Neil was mesmerised. Visiting came to an end all too quickly and Mum and Dad had to prise me away from Paul's incubator. I blew Paul a kiss and started to cry as I did not know when I would see him again. I cried all the way home, so inconsolable was I at being separated from my baby brother.

Paul stayed in hospital for a couple more weeks then, finally, we got the news we had been waiting for. On the proviso that we would bring Paul back at a later date for further treatment, we were allowed to take him home. Mum had got the basics for the baby at home: pram, carrycot, cot, nappies and a baby bath and toiletries, but she had not bought any clothes. So, before we picked Paul up, we made a visit to the baby linen shop on Holderness Road. It was just along from the high-class bakers, *Wallis's* – Mum used to buy lovely cakes and loaves of bread from Wallis's and Neil and I used to tease her about the rather posh accent she affected when ordering baked goods there. We actually called it her 'Wallis's voice'. When we moved to York, she used the same accent when talking on the phone, it really made us laugh. Poor Mum.

The baby linen shop was one I loved visiting. It always had a display of baby dresses and suits in the window and I used to covet them longingly for my bigger dolls, but they were far too expensive. Mum said that I could help her choose two little suits for baby Paul. Mum did not decide to dress Paul in all white, so we had quite a choice of pastel colours to choose from. Mum wanted two-piece shorts suits, so she could get them off quickly to change them, far more than usual, of course. She would have to change Paul many times and she did not want any rompers as they were all-in-one. The first suit we chose was mostly white with little puff sleeves. It had a small pocket on the chest and that had embroidery of little red and blue animals on it. The second one was white and lemon with short sleeves and, again, a bit of embroidery. It also had some smocking on the top – Mum liked smocking. The lemon pants had a raised pattern on them too. I liked them both, but I liked the white one best. Mum then bought a couple of white baby nightdresses in a fabric called 'Vyela'. Now we were ready to welcome Paul back home.

So, finally, after what seemed to be an age, we brought Paul home and we began to develop new routines as a family. Dad was really thrilled and happy to have his youngest child back home. He was good with babies and enjoyed taking Paul out in his big pram, rocking him to sleep and making him smile and, later, laugh. Dad used to sing a special song to me as a baby and toddler, it was a popular one, often played on the wireless in those days. It was a Rodgers and Hammerstein song from the show *Flower Drum Song.* He used to swing me around while singing: "Sunday, sweet Sunday, with nothing to do. Lazy and lovely, my one day with you. Happy and hazy, we'll drift through the day, dreaming the hours away." He knew all the words and he used to make me laugh as he swung me round. With Paul, he chose an old music hall song: "I'll be your sweetheart, if you will be mine. All my life I'll be your valentine. Bluebells I'll gather, take them and be true. When I'm a man my plan will be to marry you." Not terribly appropriate, but Dad used them to calm or amuse Paul, according to what was needed. And it was really sweet to see baby Paul respond to Dad's singing. Neil must have had his own song too, but I do not remember what it was. I will have to ask him.

As soon as Paul came home, I became like a second mother to him. I watched everything that Mum did for him and it was not long before I too was able to feed Paul with a bottle, help bath and dress him and walk him out in the Silver Cross pram. Our first walk was very exciting as people we knew came out to talk to me and take their first peep at our beautiful new baby. Some, to my surprise, opened one of his hands and pressed a half crown (2/6) into his tiny hand. It was to do with an old wives' tale to give the child luck, health and happiness in their future. It was all gratefully received and Mum put it in a piggy bank to be paid into Paul's Halifax account as soon as it was opened.

The only part of Paul being home, the thing that worried and upset Mum and I, was the ongoing treatment he required. Every nappy change, Mum had to wear special gloves and open up Paul's back passage. It was a horrible thing for Mum to have to do, but essential for Paul's future health. It was very painful and he used to scream and cry terribly. It used to make Mum really upset, one of the few times she ever shed tears was over nappy-changing times. After the ordeal was over, I was given the task of distracting Paul with toys, cuddles and peek-a-boo type games. Paul was a resilient baby and he soon got over the pain he suffered. Mum found the constant laundering of nappies a real chore though. Paul's skin was very delicate and he needed changing far more than a normal baby would.

Mum's salvation in the nappy department came from a new product someone told her about. It was called a 'Paddi roll' and it is not an exaggeration to say that it changed Mum's life. The Paddi roll was like a thin cottonwool pad on a roll. It was covered with thin cotton netting to prevent the cottonwool breaking up. It could be bought at the chemist and had been invented by a Scottish mother with several children who was trying to make her own life easier and ended up by helping thousands of other mums into the bargain. Mum used to cut a piece of the Paddi roll off and it was then put inside the cloth nappy to catch the soiling. The soiled nappy pad piece could then simply be removed and either put in the dustbin or flushed down the toilet. If used with skill, the terry nappy would not be dirty so there was less soaking and dealing with faecal matter and it stopped the harsh chemicals from the Milton Fluid (used for soaking the terry nappies) from touching Paul's sensitive skin, so, fewer rashes for him. This really was transformational as far as Mum was concerned. She must have used miles of it caring for Paul over the baby days. Mum thought it was one of the best inventions ever for babies and when she heard that the lady who invented it died just a few years ago, she was very sorry. Mum also recommended it for other mothers and I am sure it made life easier for them as well.

Dad wrote on the back of this photo "The agony and the ecstasy of a Sunday morning"

Dad liked to hang us on the swing and the winner was the one who stayed up the longest - It was usually me!

Baby Paul looks on in bewilderment

Neil, Paul and I in the garden at home.
I'm helping Paul to have a go on the swing.
I was like a little mother to him.

Outside the Newsagents with Neil and Paul.
VICTORY!! My hair is long enough for bunches.
This was taken just before the move to York.

CHAPTER 24 : The Move

This will be a very painful chapter as I feel that what happened to our family next created a rift between my early childhood and my later childhood. A watershed time that caused me to grow up very quickly as a way of coping with feelings of grief and loss as we moved from Hull – my childhood and much-loved home – to York.

Dad said he had something to tell us one night after tea. He had just got a new job. It was still a job that had something to do with the railways, but it had better promotion prospects and a better salary. Dad was moving up the career ladder – that was the good news. The bad news was that we were going to have to move away from Hull and our extended family, our street, our school and move to a new city, York. Dad said it was a beautiful and historic place and he thought that once we settled down, we would grow to love it too. To me, this was a massive bombshell. It would mean moving away from everything I loved, especially Grandma and Grandad and all my other relatives. I would lose touch with all my friends. We would have to start again with a new, different school. It all sounded really frightening; I just did not want to leave Hull, it was my home in every sense of the word. Nothing could ever compare to Hull for me.

I know that Dad was just trying to better himself and doing what he thought was best for our whole family. However, he had no idea of the effects the move would have on Neil and me. So deep were my feelings of grief and loss, unmatched by anything that had so far happened in my life, that I made a decision that would affect my own children. The move was so very painful to me that I vowed to myself that I would never move my future children's location from one place to another once they were of school age. It was so traumatic to me that I would never subject them to what I had to cope with at the tender age of 10. And I never did.

I was a full-time mum to my children and we had one move as a family, from Castle Donington to Beeston, Nottingham before my eldest child, Joshua, started school. I never regretted that decision. I grieved at the loss of my Hull home for years, and that grief became magnified at losing both Grandma and Grandad just three years later. It felt to me that all that had made me feel secure and happy had been swept away. I talked to Mum about it, but the die was cast – we *were* moving. There was nothing anyone could do and it broke my heart.

For a while, things continued in Hull as they had before with the welcome addition of our wonderful baby, Paul. I moved with all my friends from Archbishop William Temple School to a new middle school, Alderman Cogan, another Christian school. The authorities decided to change the structure from the all-in-one 5-11 primary school to 'first school' (5-8) and 'middle school' (8-13). Later in life, I trained as a teacher for the middle school system. That was why I could teach in both primary and secondary schools, and, in fact, my first teaching appointment was in a secondary school. I later taught in primary schools. The areas of England in which I worked never adopted the middle school system, but it was common in the south of England (Buckinghamshire, etc) where I did all my teaching practices.

Alderman Cogan was most definitely based on a traditional secondary/grammar school rather than a primary school. (That was a big problem for me when we moved to York as I had to go to a country-type primary school.) At Alderman Cogan we had a school uniform – very formal with a tie. We had to move around the buildings to study different subjects and we were streamed for all our main subjects. To my horror, despite being top of the class at English at Archbishop William Temple, I was now put in the 'B' class. Archbishop William Temple had been good at allowing children to express themselves through creative writing. Not so good at teaching grammar. I learned a lot about grammar in just a few months at Alderman Cogan and I saw, quite clearly, the gaps in my English education. Perhaps, though, the biggest change was in PE lessons. Mum had to buy me a special PE kit. It was no longer a case of wearing a pair of black plimsolls and dressing in your vest and knickers. Now we had navy blue shorts or skirts, short white socks and a white Airtex blouse. Girls and boys did not undress together in the classroom anymore. Each sex had their own changing rooms with showers after games sessions. We felt very adult.

This being Hull though, most of the children still went home at dinner time and as I lived quite a distance from the new school, I went on a bus to and fro – four bus journeys a day. The school was not far from Grandma and Grandad's house and they used to often come to the bus stop to have a chat before I went home. It was about two miles from Beech Avenue and cost a couple of old pennies per journey and I used to collect the Victorian pennies (I have them still). It was especially pleasing to get a 'bun' penny – the earliest Victorian penny – so called because the Queen Victoria portrait showed her hair in a bun. The later ones showed her in her widow's weeds with her veil over her hair and a sombre expression on her face. I collected quite a few of those old pennies too.

Now that there was a new baby in the house, Grandma and Grandad began to visit Mum whilst we were at school to help with the housework and to take Paul out in his pram. They were so excited about having another grandson, and Grandad seemed especially fond of baby Paul – Mum remarked on how lovely it was to see them so close together. Sometimes, Grandad used to come on his own just to take Paul out in the pram. It was something he would have missed out on with our own dad as I am sure Grandma devoted herself to little Geoffrey and Grandad would have normally been out at work while she stayed at home to look after Dad and the house. This was Grandad's chance to spend time on his own with his grandchild and he cherished every visit, especially as he knew those moments would be at an end when we moved away to York.

Grandma and Grandad were so sad that we were leaving, although I am sure they were proud of Dad's career progress and would never have tried to hold him back. However, our move would mean far less contact with their beloved grandchildren. No regular contact at all in fact, only on high days and holidays. It must have been hard for them after being used to our weekly all morning Saturday visits, plus other visits whenever we were able. They could not drive and it was expensive on the train. Also, unbeknown to us children, both Grandma and Grandad were getting older and ill. Grandad had repeated heart attacks from his mid-forties onwards, landing him in hospital. He probably had high cholesterol, but no one knew about such things in the 1960s.

As Mum and Dad had no phone in Hull, the first they knew about Grandad being in hospital was when they received Grandma's letters saying he was, yet again, in hospital. Grandma too was ill for about 15 years before she died but was too modest to tell her doctor about the blood in her urine. Dad always said she had Dr Deakin – the worst doctor in Hull who would send many patients with serious conditions away without proper help. However, Grandma trusted Dr Deakin completely and would not hear a word said against him. In those days, GP practices were often one-man bands, so there was no chance of a second opinion. If you got a duff doctor, you were stuck with them. Dr Deakin, according to Dad, was a duff GP.

Grandma was born in 1901, right at the end of Queen Victoria's reign and her upbringing with her sisters, Clarice and Amanda (Aunt Manda to us, a true old eccentric) was positively Victorian. Nothing about any personal health issues ever sullied Grandma's lips. 'Things down below' were only ever referred to with hushed whispers and Grandma only went for medical help when things were far beyond healing. To give you an idea of how ladylike Grandma was, when ordering belly pork at the butchers, she would only ever ask for 'stomach' pork as 'belly' was a vulgar word to her. Grandma was the most wonderful person: gentle, loving, modest and ladylike, the perfect model of Christian womanhood; we all adored her, especially Dad.

Grandma and Grandad (despite their infirmities at that time) tried to move house to be nearer to us in York. A stately home just outside York was advertising for a married couple to serve them. The husband would be expected to do odd jobs and work in the garden – perfect for Grandad – and the wife would be expected to cook, clean and tend to the other housework needs of the family. The best part of it was that it was a live-in position. Grandma and Grandad lived in a rented house so could not sell up and move to be near us. They had no money and rental costs were greater in York. They went for the interview but found it unsuitable as it would be far too much work at their time of life. Grandma told Mum that the family lived in the manor as if they were from a previous generation and she was especially horrified that the lady of the house and her daughter used torn up strips of sheets as sanitary towels which she would have been expected to launder and make spotless. These were hanging on rails in front of the open fire on the day of the interview. So that idea was one which had to be abandoned. Grandma and Grandad were not going to be able to move to York to be near us, we were going to have to travel back to see them regularly.

Our house was put on the market and it sold fairly quickly. I do not remember if we children saw our new home in York, but we were due to move just after the Easter school holiday. It meant that we would miss the first few days of the summer term at our new school. I well remember my sorrow at walking down the 10-foot and around Beech Avenue with my friend, Joan, pushing our dolls' prams together for the last time.

In the days before people had phones, mobiles or the internet, the only possible way of keeping in touch with friends and family was   by   writing   a letter. I just knew we would never meet again and we did not. Our old home in Hull was lost to us forever. Our lives now were elsewhere in a very different sort of place, York. Beloved of tourists, full of all sorts of history (especially Viking and Roman history), so different in character to Hull and, once we moved, we did indeed see a lot less of all our relatives. It was most definitely the end of an era for us as a family.

I went to York in great fear and trepidation for the future. The early part of my mostly carefree childhood was over and I was entering the next phase of my life at the tender age of 10.

Next Page:

The final picture of us all as a family with Grandma and Grandad on a lovely day out at Castle Howard, just before the move to York.

Acknowledgements

Heart-felt thanks go to Julia Vaughan for working so hard typing up the manuscript from my Cassette recordings – without you there wouldn't be a book!

Thanks also go to my friends at the Denison Street Book Group – not only did you listen to early extracts, but you also gave me the encouragement I needed to finish the work.

Similarly, thanks go to The Rev. Paul Reynolds who also encouraged me to complete this book after I read an extract of an early draft at the Post COVID Church Social at St Michael and All Angels, Bramcote.

And last (and by no means least): to Andrew, my supportive husband, for your help liaising with Julia, helping with edits, copying and placing the photographs, and setting up the book for printing

WS - #0083 - 100625 - C12 - 210/148/11 [13] - CB - 9781836903321 - Gloss Lamination